by LINDA HARRISON

starting points

Creating meaningful scrapbook layouts from whatever inspires you

MEMORY MAKERS BOOKS

Cincinnati, Ohio
www.mycraftivity.com

About the *author*

Linda Harrison's love for design, color, photography and storytelling all unite to form her passion for scrapbooking and papercrafting. Linda has been creating in some form or another since she was a child. In 2005 she took her creating to another level when she began doing freelance work in the craft industry. She has since designed for a variety of manufacturers and has had her work published in several publications. Linda was inducted into the 2007 Creating Keepsakes Hall of Fame and was featured as a Scrapbook Trends Trendsetter for 2006. When she's not creating, Linda enjoys filling her days with fun family times with her husband and son, reading and enjoying the beaches in her hometown of Sarasota, Florida.

Starting Points. Copyright© 2008 by Linda Harrison. Manufactured in China. All rights reserved. It is permissible for the purchaser to make the projects contained herein and sell them at fairs, bazaars and craft shows. No other part of this book may be reproduced in any form or by any electronic or mechanical means including information storage and retrieval systems without permission in writing from the publisher, except by a reviewer, who may quote a brief passage in review. Published by Memory Makers Books, an imprint of F+W Publications, Inc., 4700 East Galbraith Road, Cincinnati, Ohio 45236. (800) 289-0963. First edition.

12 11 10 09 08 5 4 3 2 1

Distributed in Canada by Fraser Direct
100 Armstrong Avenue
Georgetown, ON, Canada L7G 5S4
Tel: (905) 877-4411

Distributed in the U.K. and Europe by David & Charles
Brunel House, Newton Abbot, Devon, TQ12 4PU, England
Tel: (+44) 1626 323200, Fax: (+44) 1626 323319
E-mail: postmaster@davidandcharles.co.uk

Distributed in Australia by Capricorn Link
P.O. Box 704, S. Windsor, NSW 2756 Australia
Tel: (02) 4577-3555

Library of Congress Cataloging-in-Publication Data

Harrison, Linda, scrapbooker.
    Starting points : creating meaningful scrapbook layouts from whatever inspires you / Linda Harrison. -- 1st ed.
       p. cm.
    Includes index.
    ISBN 978-1-59963-026-7 (pbk. : alk. paper)
    1. Photograph albums. 2. Scrapbooks. I. Title.
TR501.H376 2008
745.593--dc22
                              2008002822

○ ○ Metric Conversion Chart ○ ○

to convert	to	multiply by
Inches	Centimeters	2.54
Centimeters	Inches	0.4
Feet	Centimeters	30.5
Centimeters	Feet	0.03
Yards	Meters	0.9
Meters	Yards	1.1
Sq. Inches	Sq. Centimeters	6.45
Sq. Centimeters	Sq. Inches	0.16
Sq. Feet	Sq. Meters	0.09
Sq. Meters	Sq. Feet	10.8
Sq. Yards	Sq. Meters	0.8
Sq. Meters	Sq. Yards	1.2
Pounds	Kilograms	0.45
Kilograms	Pounds	2.2
Ounces	Grams	28.3
Grams	Ounces	0.035

fw
F+W PUBLICATIONS, INC.
www.fwpublications.com

Editor *Kristin Boys*
Designer *Kelly O'Dell*
Art Coordinator *Eileen Aber*
Production Coordinator *Matt Wagner*
Photographers *Ric Deliantoni*
                     Tim Grondin
Stylist *Nora Martini*

I always envisioned the process of writing a book was a bit of a lonely one, as an author works to mold her thoughts into a finished product. However, I was very wrong. There were so many people who played a part in my creating this book. Without their gift of time and support, I would have never been able to finish.

My hugest appreciation goes to *my husband, Rob*. Your never-ending support, patience and ability to take over with things when I lacked time was amazing. You are the reason I was able to take on this book in the first place. If you weren't there to do everything else in our life as needed, this book wouldn't have been possible. My appreciation and love for you is beyond measure. Thank you for all you do and for the wonderful person you are. I love you. And to *my little guy, Robby*, who gave me support beyond what I thought his four years was capable. Thank you, Sweetie for your understanding of Mommy's changing schedule and your innocent and constant interest in the "pretty things" that Mommy creates. I love you and hope that you enjoy looking at all of Mommy's pretties in one place.

To my mom and my dad, you did the impossible and allowed me to create more time in my days. Thank you for being there when I needed more. I also wouldn't have the luxury of doing this without all that you have given me. Thank you for continuing to encourage me as I make my way though the rest of my life. I love you both. And to *the rest of my family* who were there to take over and encourage when they have lives even busier than mine. Thank you for taking time out of your days to add a little to mine. I appreciate it more than you know and wouldn't have been able to do this without you. Thank you for your interest in what I do. I love you guys.

To my friends, thank you for your patience and your encouragement. To my friends who don't scrapbook, I thank you for allowing me to fill my time with something that means so much to me, and still be there to encourage. To my scrapbook friends, especially *Summer* and *Kim*, thank you for your interest, support and patience as the writing of this book became my focus for so many months. You two put up with it more than any, but without the constant encouragement from everyone, this could've become a very lonely process. Thank you for not letting it.

To my contributors, thank you! Thank you for your contributions and for making this book so much more interesting and pretty than if your work wasn't inside. I will treasure the time and art you have shared with me and those who read this book. Thank you.

I want to send a special thank you to *Kathleen Summers, Paul* and *Kezia Whitteker, Kim Moreno, Tara Tuck, Wendy White* and *the team at www.scrapsupply.com,* for bearing with me as I used the time I would normally be creating for them, creating for this book. Your support and patience during the process did not go unnoticed.

Finally, I want to thank the wonderful women at *Memory Makers Books* for being such a breeze to work with. Thank you *Christine Doyle* for encouraging me to begin this process. I am forever grateful to you for giving me the push to get my thoughts and artwork in book form. And thank you to *Kristin Boys* for being so incredibly easy to work with and for making my rough version into the beauty it is today. Thank you to everyone who played a part in getting the book to this final product.

8

1

Now that captures it!
Starting your pages with photos

36

2

Wait until you read this!
Starting your pages with words

When mom took me to Europe for a graduation present, I was thrill I love to travel and was excited at the chance to visit so many exciting countries and spend quality time with mom. The interesting thing about the tr been how it has affected since returning. Although took place almost ten year's I am still benefiting from The remembrance of the jo fortunes to warm my ___ ___ ies of thi

my favorite **treat**

POPCORN

makes me *smile*

love

meant

Don't you just love it ? 3
Starting your pages with product

Doesn't that look interesting ? 4
Starting your pages with other inspirations

FINDING YOUR STARTING POINT

Now that I've been creating scrapbook pages for so many years, I really can't pinpoint how it all began. I know I started doing it more in college and that I've been more consistent with it since my son's birth. However, now that scrapbooking the memories of my life are second-nature, it is hard to picture at what point it started.

Even though I have a hard time remembering exactly when my love for scrapbooking began, I do recall how each and every one of my layouts started. When I look at any layout in my albums, the first thing that hits me is the starting point. My starting point is something that no one else would know, or even care to notice, but it is what I see first. What does this mean? It means that I can recognize what inspired me to do that layout in the first place. Inspiration is the birth of an idea that grows and completes itself on a layout.

A starting point—the inspiration or catalyst—for creating a layout can come from anywhere. I have been inspired to create pages for my albums for a number of reasons. I have come across old photos that I just had to scrap for my own albums. I have had conversations that I just had to document. I have acquired some gorgeous products, and I have noticed things around me that inspired me to create.

I hope this book helps you find your own starting points. I hope it teaches you to recognize why you want to create a page and then how to make that page meaningful and attractive based on a particular starting point. Most of all, I hope you are inspired to create, whatever your starting point may be.

red shoes

blue shoes

j

s

It was time for your first season of 'coach-pitch' baseball! Red cleats for Joey, blue for Sammy. Not only were they a perfect match for the uniform, but also totally helped coach Rob to tell you two apart! 2005

Now that captures it!

Starting your pages with photos

Most of us start to scrapbook because we have photos that we just have to share, those that seem to call for more than just a frame and glass. It's no wonder that photos become the starting point for so many of the layouts that we scrapbook. So, how do you use your photos to create a meaningful layout? In this chapter, I'll show you a variety of layouts that started with photos. You'll see how to design a layout around a photo, how to make a photo the star of your page and how to look at your photos differently. Before you know it, creating a layout from a starting point photo will be as easy as finding a photo to scrap.

Some say photos are more interesting if you get people in your pictures. Here, Ali proves that's not always the case. Using photos of the colors, sights, signs and textures of a vacation location can create a really interesting page. A two-page layout with lots of small photos will really showcase your scenic shots.

Artwork by Ali McLaughlin

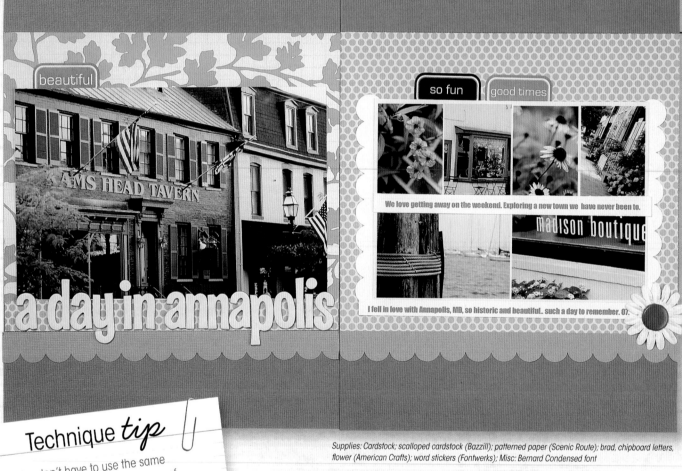

Technique *tip*

You don't have to use the same patterned paper on both pages of a two-page layout. Just incorporate similar colors and add an element that spans both pages to unify them.

Supplies: Cardstock; scalloped cardstock (Bazzill); patterned paper (Scenic Route); brad, chipboard letters, flower (American Crafts); word stickers (Fontwerks); Misc: Bernard Condensed font

STARTING POINT

my favorite

treat

Yum!

popcorn is by far my favorite treat. I cave every single time I get a whiff of that delicious, fresh-popped, butter-and-salted goodness.

Yum!

enjoy

eat

delicious

POPCORN
FRESH

Supplies: Cardstock; patterned paper (KI Memories); chipboard letters (Imagination Project); chipboard accents (Heidi Swapp, KI Memories); die-cut letters and shapes (QuicKutz); metal word (Making Memories); paper frills (Doodlebug); raised circles (Chatterbox); Misc: 2peas High Tide font, corner rounder

I love popcorn! So it wasn't a huge surprise when I found this photo in with others I took during a vacation. When taking photos, don't forget to turn the camera away from your family to capture other things around you. You could end up with a photo that's a great starting place for a layout all about something you love.

STARTING POINT

POPCORN
FRESH

---

a Different memory

It's not so much that I was surprised to see a computer in our hotel room. I had traveled quite a lot the previous year for 'work' and would've loved to have had a computer in one of my hotel rooms instead of just a cord to connect my laptop. So it isn't that I'm not used to technology seeping into my travels. I think it hit me harder because we were at Disney. Walt Disney World to be exact. And being at Disney for the first time with you brought back so many of my own childhood Disney memories. None of which ever included a computer. Or a cell phone. Or any of the modern technologies that we now seem unable to escape, even when vacationing. I've never been one to curse technology or dwell too much on how things used to be, but I must admit that seeing you playing games online in our hotel room is not what I had pictured happening during our Disney vacation. It didn't bother me that you were doing it, it was just bittersweet to know that I didn't have a comparable childhood memory to compare it to. It made it too obvious for comfort that the world has definitely changed since I was a child and it made it way to clear that I am getting older. These are your childhood memories, though, not mine, and I appreciate them for what they are and how you will look back and see them when you are my age. And who knows what you own children will be doing at Disney then! I can only imagine!

May WDW 2007

When I first took these photos, it was to record what my son was experiencing during our first trip to Disney World. What I didn't realize was that seeing these photos later would spark memories of my own trip as a kid and how things have changed since then. Use photos of your kids to prompt layouts about your own childhood.

STARTING POINT

Supplies: Cardstock; die-cut letters (QuicKutz); chipboard accent (Scenic Route); metal accents (7gypsies); brads (Making Memories); Misc: Georgia font, circle punch

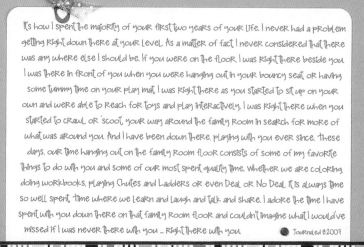

It's how I spent the majority of your first two years of your life. I never had a problem getting right down there at your level. As a matter of fact I never considered that there was any where else I should be. If you were on the floor, I was right there beside you. I was there in front of you when you were hanging out in your bouncy seat or having some tummy time on your play mat. I was right there as you started to sit up on your own and were able to reach for toys and play interactively. I was right there when you started to crawl, or 'scoot', your way around the family room in search for more of what was around you. And I have been down there, playing with you ever since. these days, our time hanging out on the family room floor consists of some of my favorite things to do with you and some of our most spent quality time. Whether we are coloring, doing workbooks, playing Chutes and Ladders or even Deal or No Deal, it is always time so well spent, time where we learn and laugh and talk and share. I adore the time I have spent with you down there on that family room floor and couldn't imagine what I would've missed if I was never there with you ... right there with you

● Journaled 8.2007

on the
Down Low

Supplies: Cardstock; brads, letter stickers, patterned paper (American Crafts); chipboard letters (Heidi Swapp); bookplate (BasicGrey); clip (Making Memories); ribbon (SEI); Misc: SP Sara Jean font, corner rounder

I took this self-portrait when I was testing my camera's timer. As I was looking at the picture, I realized this was how I am usually seen by my son—we spend lots of time on the floor together. Lesson learned: A "practice" photo can be a great starting point for a meaningful layout.

STARTING POINT

Technique *tip*

Learn how to use the self-timer on your camera. It will allow you to take more photos of you as well as photos of your family that actually have everyone in them.

Artwork by Ali McLaughlin

what a difference a year makes.

then

Almost a year has gone by since we got you. You are still as active as ever.. you almost have the pottytraining down. You are attatched to us as ever, we can't imagine not having you in our life. August 2007.

Technique *tip*

Choose the same day each year to take a photo of each family member to record everyone's changes from year to year.

Supplies: Cardstock; button, patterned paper (American Crafts); flower (KI Memories); arrows (Heidi Swapp); Misc: Arial font

It is always amazing to witness how fast time flies and how quickly our kids, and pets, grow. In this delightful layout, Ali shows how much her family's dog has grown over the past year. Recording change is an essential way to keep track of life on our layouts. Remember to take photos at different points in time and create a layout with photos side by side to show change.

STARTING POINT

The Final Approach

I didn't know it at the time. How could I have? After all, I had already taken at least 20 photos of you at the park that morning. So why would this photo be any different than the rest? I didn't always take the camera with us places, but on this morning I did, and took advantage of the empty playground to snap away. You didn't even seem to notice me as you ran from activity to activity. You kept busy climbing and sliding and running and swinging. I captured this photo of you running for the toddler swings without a thought. Just another photo of you running to another activity. Or was it? A few days later, when I printed this photo, I realized that this wasn't an ordinary photo. For me, this was one of those pictures of you that would speak to me, without need for words. One of those photos that emerged every now and again that manage to capture a moment frozen. For me, I knew this photo would capture one of the last times that you would be running to those toddler swings. You hadn't begun to swing on the big swings by yourself yet, but I knew it was coming and I knew when it did, that I would look back at this photo with a bittersweet appreciation. Another activity outgrown; another moment frozen in time.

I hung onto this photo for a while before I could properly pair it with words. Once I realized this was the last photo of my son at the toddler swings, I knew I had captured a precious time. This photo became the starting point to let out how I was feeling about my son getting older. Use photos from different stages of your child's growth to prompt thoughts for a layout.

Supplies: Cardstock; die-cut letters and shapes (QuicKutz); brads (Making Memories); date sticker (EK Success); buttons (Jo-Ann's); digital journaling template by Kellie Mize (Designer Digitals); Misc: Arial font

Technique *tip*

If you have a lot of journaling on a simply designed page, type it up and then print it directly onto your cardstock. This will help the journaling flow with the rest of the design.

STARTING POINT

Believe it or not, there was a time that most of us didn't take as many photos as we do now that digital cameras are so popular. Unfortunately, my pregnancy was one of those times. So I have to get creative when showing pregnancy pictures. This photo was meant to record a trip to New York until I realized that this was one of a few photos of my pregnancy. It's a lesson to look at all my photos with a different eye.

Supplies: Cardstock; patterned paper (Reminisce); chipboard letters, felt flowers, letter stickers (American Crafts); die-cut thought bubble (QuicKutz); eyelets (Making Memories); Misc: Traveling Typewriter font

This is one of those photos that fills me with emotion every time I see it, and yet by looking it you would never know why. On the surface, it is a picture of me in front of City Hall in Southampton, New York. It was taken during a trip up there after Rob and I had already moved to Florida. On this day we were visiting the streets of Southampton, remembering where I used to work and where we used to eat, and any other memories that came to us of our time spent there before. I asked Rob to take this photo of me here because I used to walk into that building quite frequently when I worked at a law office across the street. That's all this photo was supposed to be. However, what it means to me now is something all together different. At the time of this photo, I was around three months pregnant with Robby. I didn't know it at the time, but this would be one of only a few photos that we took of me while I was pregnant. So now every time I see this photo that is ALL I can see is that this is me carrying Robby...and I LOVE that. This is one of those photos that reminds me to keep on taking pictures throughout our lives no matter what the occasion. You never know what they can come to mean later and I have yet to have the thought that I had too many pictures of any one time in our lives. In this case, I definitely had too few.

Photo: 2002 / Journaling: 2008

ONE of FEW

ROBBY WAS HERE!

STARTING POINT

How to *Capture* it

If you want to start your pages with photos, you're going to need some photos! Even if you have an expensive SLR (single-lens reflex) or digital-SLR that you tote with you to events and occasions, it helps to have a reliable point-and-shoot that you can keep in your bag at all times. You never know when you may want to snap a photo as you pick your child up from school or when you run into a friend and end up going for a cup of coffee. My point-and-shoot has been the camera for many everyday-type shots that I would be sad to have missed.

'07

MEMORIES

grandpa

Every summer we make a point to take a family road trip up to Grandpa's summer home in the mountains of North Carolina. Do we do it to take a vacation from Florida? Sure. Is it to relax in the beautiful mountains? You bet. But there is no bigger reason for making that annual road trip than the chance to come home with memories like this. June 2007

time with **papa**

Supplies: Cardstock; patterned paper (Fontwerks); chipboard letters and numbers (Heidi Swapp); brads, letter stickers (Making Memories); word stickers (7gypsies); bookplate, rub-on (BasicGrey); chipboard circle (Bazzill); Misc: Incogni-type font, paint

With the aid of digital editing and zoom lenses, it's easy to get used to framing photos just around your subjects. But looking at a photo's original composition can be a great place to begin a layout. The background in this photo, rather than the subject, inspired my layout design—quiet and calm, rustic and classic, with shades of red and gray. When using a photo to inspire a layout, try looking behind the subject for a place to start.

STARTING POINT

Technique *tip*

If you want to use a photo with lots of background but the details are a bit too small, simply enlarge your photo and use it as the perfect backdrop for your layout.

Artwork by Kelly Noel

Supplies: Cardstock (Bazzill); patterned paper (Scenic Route); chipboard letters (Heidi Swapp); buttons, chipboard heart, ribbon (American Crafts); label sticker (Making Memories); rub-on (Autumn Leaves); Misc: Kayleigh font

Kelly's layout flawlessly conveys why it isn't always necessary to get that perfect shot of your subject smiling at the camera. Capturing partial shots of your subjects at play can express as much emotion as any big smile. Look for those less-than-perfect photos to start scrapping layouts that add variety and interest to your albums.

STARTING POINT

STARTING POINT

It is such a treat when we capture our loved ones as we usually see them. We don't always see people perfectly posed with smiles, so why only have photos that represent that? Take photos of your family and friends in natural settings so that you have starting points for pages recording real life.

Supplies: Cardstock; chipboard letters, ribbon (BoBunny); stamps (Inque Boutique); straight pins (Fancy Pants); buttons (Jo-Ann's); Misc: ink, paint

It isn't how we ideally begin our day. Especially a holiday. But even daddy and I realize the basketful of temptation you woke to that one Easter morning was just too much to take. You are always so good about saving your snacks for after meals, but when a bunny brings you a bright blue lollipop in the morning, how can you resist?

LIFE SAVER

EASTER breakfast ?

Holidays tend to go by in a blur, so I was happy to have captured these photos of my son wasting no time diving into his Easter basket. Without these photos, the memory of this Easter breakfast would've soon been forgotten. With photos, even a little moment can become a great place to start a layout. Always have your camera ready and clicking to create great starting points for your holiday pages.

Supplies: Cardstock; patterned paper, rub-on (American Crafts); letter stickers (American Crafts, BasicGrey); rickrack (Maya Road); paper frills (Doodlebug); Misc: Love Ya Like A Sister font

Technique *tip*

Even when you think you have captured the perfect photo, keep snapping! A series of photos is often more telling and interesting than a single picture.

STARTING POINT

Artwork by Denine Zielinski

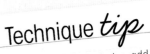

STARTING POINT

When I look at this layout, there is no question that this handsome smiling boy is celebrating a birthday. Denine did a fabulous job creating a festive birthday page without the need for photos of presents, cake, decorations or guests. If all you to have to start a page is one close-up photo during a celebration, you can still create a fabulously festive layout marking the occasion.

Supplies: Cardstock; patterned paper (Arctic Frog, KI Memories); rub-on words (Beary Patch, Scenic Route, Wordsworth); letter stickers (American Crafts); grommets (Making Memories); accent stickers (KI Memories, Pebbles); Misc: Cammie Pea font, felt

Technique *tip*

To make up for fewer photos, add fun, bright and festive-colored embellishments that make a layout feel like one big party.

iF YOU GiVE a KiD a CameRa...

YOU'LL SEE THE WORLD **THROUGH HiS eyes**

ALL PHOTOS BY HOLDEN (AGE 4) AND SCARLETT (AGE 6)

Artwork by Lisa Moorefield

As scrapbookers, we tend to take a lot of pictures. So it's no wonder that our kids would take an early interest in the camera. On this precious layout, Lisa highlighted snapshots taken by her kids. Hand over your own camera to your kids and use their photos as inspiration for your layouts.

Supplies: Cardstock; patterned paper (Imaginisce); Misc: Café Rojo font

STARTING POINT

I am a glass half-full, rose-colored sunglass wearing, looking on the

Optimist

bright side of things, positive thinking type of gal.

Supplies: Cardstock; Misc: Ligurino font, buttons, floss

STARTING POINT

I've always liked how this photo captures my playful and laid-back personality. But I've never scrapped it because of the slight blur. By printing the photo onto textured white cardstock, it not only minimized the blur, but made for a unique way to start a layout.

I don't go out of my way to get photos without my son's head. It's usually a result of him moving faster than I do. This time it worked out wonderfully. I fell in love with this photo and, without a head, it made cutting out the photo easy. Take advantage of partial photos as the perfect starting point to create a silhouette on a layout.

STARTING POINT

FRONT YARD EASTER EGG HUNTS STARTED WHEN YOU WERE TWO-YEARS OLD. JUST BECAUSE YOU ARE THE ONLY CHILD IN THE HOUSE, IT DOESN'T MEAN THE EASTER BUNNY DOESN'T COME.

the Hunt

AND BEING THE ONLY ONE DOING THE HUNTING DOESN'T TAKE A THING AWAY FROM THE HUNT. IF ANYTHING, IT MAKES IT MORE ENJOYABLE AS YOU ARE ABLE TO HUNT AT YOUR OWN PACE. WHO KNEW HOLIDAYS COULD BE SO MUCH FUN!

Supplies: Cardstock; Misc: Asenine font

>>>>>>>>>>>>>>>

I SAY

I started blogging in 2005. I don't remember the exact month because at one point I shut the blog down. That didn't last long though, because soon after I had one up and running once again. In 2006 and 2007 I went though phases of posting regularly and phases where I didn't post much at all. It all related to how busy I was with life and design work. In 2008, I am making a HUGE effort to be a regular blogger. Not for any reason except that I think it is a great way to record random photos, inspirations and thoughts as they occur. Now that I am in a good groove with it, I hope to keep it going for as long as I can. 2008

ON THIS DAY: ▶

THIS IS ALL ABOUT ME WHO I AM AND WHAT I AM ALL ABOUT. WHO I LOVE AND WHAT I DO. MY DREAMS. MY HOPES. MY REALITY. MY JOYS. I DON'T EVER WANT TO FORGET THE REAL ME. THIS IS ALL ABOUT ME. IN MY OWN WORDS.

<<<<<<<<<<<

Most of us use the computer daily yet don't think to make a record of what it is we do with it. Whether it is related to work, school or entertainment, take a screen shot of a Web site or program that you often use. It may seem like an odd photo to scrap, but years from now, it will be neat to look back and see a familiar sight that may no longer be a part of what you typically do.

Supplies: Cardstock; patterned paper (Scenic Route, We R Memory Keepers); die-cut letters (QuicKutz); transparent letters (Maya Road); rub-ons (Fontwerks); bookplate (KI Memories); brads (Making Memories); Misc: Traveling Typewriter font

STARTING POINT

Technique *tip*

Search *screen shots* online for free software that allows you to easily capture a photo of your computer screen. Save the image for scrapping it. Better yet, save a bunch and make a mini album of all your favorite online sites.

One thing I have enjoyed about living in Sarasota over the years, is the city's involvement in the arts. Art fairs and exhibits are often found in town and are always a pleasure to visit and view. By far our favorite display to date came during the city's Season of Sculpture display. It featured 26 original works of art which were displayed along Sarasota Bay from November 13, 2005 – May 31, 2006. The most viewed piece, and our absolute favorite, was the "Unconditional Surrender" sculpture. This sculpture by J. Seward Johnson is based on the famous World War II photo of a sailor kissing a nurse. This 25-foot statue really made an impression every time we drove by. One day we made a point to stop and take a few photos of this bigger-than-life treat. It was so amazingly well done. As of now, it no longer sits along our bay here in Sarasota, but we sure did enjoy its beauty while it did.

Photos taken: March 12, 2006

unconditional
surrender

Supplies: Cardstock; patterned paper (Three Bugs in a Rug); die-cut letters (QuicKutz); Misc: Times New Roman font

For living in such a beautiful place, I know I don't take enough photos of the sights around my town. For this layout, an outdoor art exhibit served as inspiration for me to get out with the camera and take photos of something other than loved ones. Take a visual tour of your own town to capture the beautiful sights.

STARTING POINT

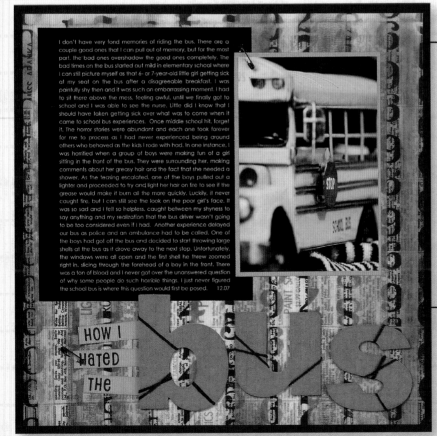

I don't have very fond memories of riding the bus. There are a couple good ones that I can pull out of memory, but for the most part, the bad ones overshadow the good ones completely. The bad times on the bus started out mild in elementary school where I can still picture myself as that 6- or 7-year-old little girl getting sick at my seat on the bus after a disagreeable breakfast. I was painfully shy then and it was such an embarrassing moment. I had to sit there above the mess, feeling awful, until we finally got to school and I was able to see the nurse. Little did I know that I should have taken getting sick over what was to come when it came to school bus experiences. Once middle school hit, forget it. The horror stories were abundant and each one took forever for me to process as I had never experienced being around others who behaved as the kids I rode with had. In one instance, I was horrified when a group of boys were making fun of a girl sitting in the front of the bus. They were surrounding her, making comments about her greasy hair and the fact that she needed a shower. As the teasing escalated, one of the boys pulled out a lighter and proceeded to try and light her hair on fire to see if the grease would make it burn all the more quickly. Luckily, it never caught fire, but I can still see the look on the poor girl's face. It was so sad and I felt so helpless, caught between my shyness to say anything and my realization that the bus driver wasn't going to be too considered even if I had. Another experience delayed our bus as police and an ambulance had to be called. One of the boys had got off the bus and decided to start throwing large shells at the bus as it drove away to the next stop. Unfortunately, the windows were all open and the first shell he threw zoomed right in, slicing through the forehead of a boy in the front. There was a ton of blood and I never got over the unanswered question of why some people do such horrible things. I just never figured the school bus is where this question would first be posed. 12.07

HOW I
HATED
THE
bus

Periodically, I take random photos of items in my son's bedroom. After seeing this photo I took of a metal school bus, memories of my school bus experiences came flooding out. Taking photos of random items in your home not only documents family life, but may spark memories for a layout.

Supplies: Cardstock; cardboard letters, patterned paper (Rusty Pickle); letter stamps (Inque Boutique); safety pins (KI Memories); Misc: Teen font, floss, ink

STARTING POINT

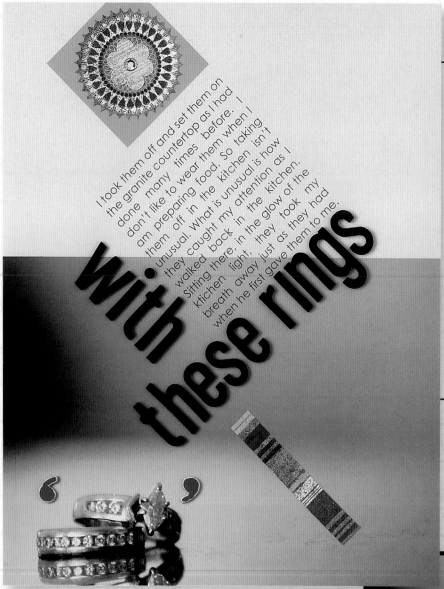

I took them off and set them on the granite countertop as I had done many times before. I don't like to wear them when I am preparing food. So taking them off in the kitchen isn't unusual. What is unusual is how they caught my attention as I walked back in the kitchen. Sitting there, in the glow of the kitchen light, they took my breath away just as they had when he first gave them to me.

with these rings

I snapped a photo of these rings after a quick glance brought about a rush of emotions. At the time, I didn't know what I'd do with the photo, but I took it anyway, and now I have a beautifully meaningful page. Taking pictures of things around you may seem unimportant, but you may never know when they will inspire a layout.

Supplies: Cardstock; patterned paper (BasicGrey); chipboard quotations, letter stickers (American Crafts); rhinestones (Me & My Big Ideas); digital template by Kellie Mize (Designer Digitals); Misc: Century Gothic font

STARTING POINT

Technique *tip*

Don't be afraid to bring the rest of your layout onto your photo. The use of quotation marks or other symbols can help bring attention to the subject of your photo.

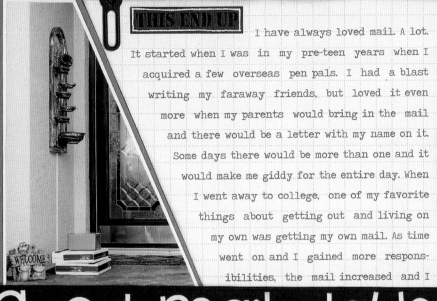

THIS END UP

I have always loved mail. A lot. It started when I was in my pre-teen years when I acquired a few overseas pen pals. I had a blast writing my faraway friends, but loved it even more when my parents would bring in the mail and there would be a letter with my name on it. Some days there would be more than one and it would make me giddy for the entire day. When I went away to college, one of my favorite things about getting out and living on my own was getting my own mail. As time went on and I gained more responsibilities, the mail increased and I

good · mail · days

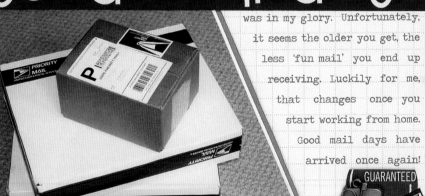

was in my glory. Unfortunately, it seems the older you get, the less 'fun mail' you end up receiving. Luckily for me, that changes once you start working from home. Good mail days have arrived once again!

GUARANTEED
SPECIAL DELIVERY

Supplies: Cardstock; letter stickers (Doodlebug); brads (American Crafts); photo turn, rub-on, sticker accent (7gypsies); metal charm (Karen Foster); Misc: Traveling Typewriter font, circle punch

Boxes at my doorstep have become a familiar sight as I continue to be an at-home designer. Working from home means using postal and delivery services to get things in and out of my studio. It only made sense to capture this familiar image and use it as a starting point for a layout. Make a point to capture familiar sights of your day and be inspired to create a layout about the daily happenings in your life.

Technique *tip*

For one entire day, take a photo of different things that remind you of your daily life. Here are some ideas: time on the alarm clock when you open your eyes; coffee being brewed; start of a favorite TV show; the computer screen with your e-mail; your dinner.

STARTING POINT

Harvest Gold

... And to think that all this time, I thought I didn't like yellow because of how it looked with my hair and skin. Looking back, now I see that there **is** a possibility that maybe, just maybe, I got a little tired of wearing it? I have to admit to liking what these photos represent, though. My attire certainly accurately portrays what was popular in the early 70s. Harvest gold and Avocado green were unquestionably the 'it' colors. So although today I would say that dark yellow is anything but my color, it's nice to see that at least I was always on trend.

I was inspired to create this layout after finding a common element among several childhood photos. Finding a common element in these photos allowed me a new way to scrap pictures. I would have normally scrapped one at a time or grouped by occasion. When looking for layout inspiration, gather a large group of photos and look for common elements.

Supplies: Cardstock; patterned paper (Making Memories, SEI); buttons (Autumn Leaves); Misc: Puritan Swash, Rina and Verdana fonts, corner rounder

STARTING POINT

Technique *tip*

Keep in mind the era of your photos when choosing color and embellishments. Both can be used to enhance the mood in which the photos were taken.

Artwork by Summer Fullerton

they call me Summer

©1972

Just by hearing my name most people guess I am a product of the 70's and they are right. The 70's couldn't have been a more distinguishable decade with its bold colors and wild patterns. No one embraced this time more creativity than my mom. She thought the children's clothes found in stores were boring and bland. She turned to her sewing machine and the textiles that made the 1970's so famous: making many of my clothes by hand. She dressed me in funky combinations of store bought boy's clothes and her own one of a kind creations.

By the looks of my shirt in these photos my mom added the floral appliqué and I know she didn't buy those pants in any store. Thanks to my mom I was unique even at the age of 2.

I adore this layout Summer created about herself as a child. If it warms my heart, I can imagine how much her family appreciates it. Often, those of us who scrapbook forget to put as much of ourselves on our layouts as we do our loved ones. Dig out those childhood photos, and you'll have a much appreciated starting point for your next layout.

Supplies: Cardstock; embellishment, patterned paper (Tinkering Ink); felt flowers (American Crafts); chipboard numbers and symbol (BasicGrey); rub-ons (Heidi Grace); Misc: AvantGarde font, floss, paint, staples

STARTING POINT

Technique *tip*

Keep in mind the option of turning color photos to black and white using image-editing software. While I am a fan of remembering events and people in color, there are times that making a photo black and white enhances it and tunes out distracting backgrounds or annoying colors.

Artwork by Kelly Noel

Technique *tip*

The cleaner the photo, the easier it is to have a busy background. Turning the photo to black and white will help make any photo simpler.

this

makes me smile

I never imagined how much I would enjoy watching the two of you together. You share a special bond that only brothers can share. Jackson, you are so loving and caring with your baby brother. And Brady, nobody can make you smile or laugh hysterically the way your big brother can. This picture makes me smile because it's obvious you are both so happy to have one another!

STARTING POINT

I really enjoy a crisp, clean photo that showcases the faces of those that I love. On this layout, Kelly's adorable picture of her two little guys perfectly captures their precious smiles. The great thing about starting with a photo this clean and simple on your layout is almost anything goes for the background, and the photo will still be the star of the show.

Supplies: Cardstock; die-cut shape, patterned paper (Scenic Route); brad, letter stickers, ribbon, rub-on letters (American Crafts); chipboard brackets (Heidi Swapp); Misc: Kayleigh font, tag

During the first two years of your life, going to Gymboree was one of your favorite things to do. Depending on what age you were depended on what day and time we would be there for a class. Your age also determined what was your favorite thing about Gymboree at that specific time. One thing that remained pretty constant throughout our Gymboree experience was your love for Saturdays, because that meant that it was a day daddy could go and that was cool!

Technique *tip*

Colors in your page design don't always have to "match" those in the photos. Choosing colors that complement those in your photos (such as using red with green or orange with blue) will make your photos pop.

STARTING POINT

With its colors and cool design, this photo of my husband and son peeking out the end of a toddler tunnel has always been a favorite. When I finally went to scrapbook this photo, I knew it would be the starting point for how the design of my page would take shape. Look for photos with designs or elements that you can extend beyond the photo and onto your layout.

Supplies: Cardstock; letter stickers (Dream Street); Misc: Century Gothic font

Technique *tip*

When printing lots of photos on one layout, arrange them first in an image-editing software program and then print them all at once.

When looking for the perfect design for this layout, a starting point was right in front of me! I took the ribbon my son was playing with in the photos and cut it into small strips to use on my page. Stuck for inspiration? Look within your photos for embellishment inspiration.

Supplies: Cardstock; patterned paper (KI Memories, Rusty Pickle); letter stickers (American Crafts); brads (Making Memories); Misc: Century Gothic font, gift wrap ribbon

STARTING POINT

It only took you

one day

and

one lap

around the block

to get the

confidence you needed

to ride your new bike.

If you get

this far in one day,

I can't wait to see what

you can accomplish

in a lifetime.

Supplies: Photo paper; chipboard letters (Heidi Swapp); brad, sticker accents (BoBunny); Misc: Traveling Typewriter font

There was a time that I would crop in as close as possible to a subject in a photo, but now I am inspired by open space. Here, I used it as the starting point for the layout. By printing the photo at 8.5" × 11" (22cm × 28cm), I was able to add my journaling, title and embellishments directly to the photo.

STARTING POINT

Artwork by Kelly Noel

Kelly took her busy photos into consideration when starting this lively layout. By keeping the background solid, there is nothing left to fight with the photos, which pop from her page. Life is busy, but busy photos don't have to stop you from creating a great looking layout.

Supplies: Cardstock; buttons, patterned paper (American Crafts); letter stickers (American Crafts, SEI); chipboard flower (Fancy Pants); Misc: National Primary font

STARTING POINT

Easter basket

Artwork by Amy Licht

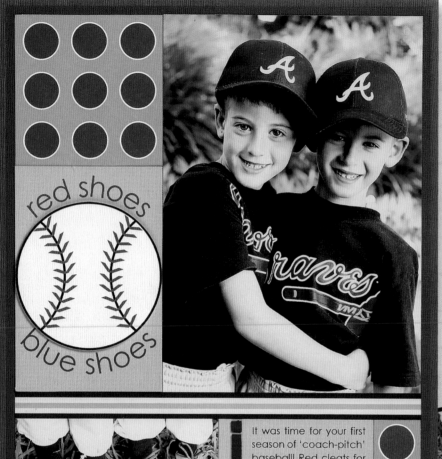

red shoes

blue shoes

J S It was time for your first season of 'coach-pitch' baseball! Red cleats for Joey, blue for Sammy. Not only were they a perfect match for the uniform, but also totally helped coach Rob to tell you two apart! 2005

STARTING POINT

An inspired layout about a special relationship doesn't have to start with a photo of the people. Amy created this super cute layout after starting with a photo of her sons' shoes, making the focus of the layout the story behind the shoes. Photos that demonstrate a relationship without showing the subjects involved can inspire a story that might not otherwise be told.

Supplies: Cardstock; patterned paper (Scenic Route); chipboard letters, decorative tape (Heidi Swapp); Misc: Century Gothic font, paint

How to Capture it

So you have some photos that have sparked an idea for a page. What happens when you're stumped about how to arrange those photos on a layout? Sketches are great starting points for designing layouts with photos. You can find sketches with one photo, two or several. Check out scrapbooking Web sites and magazines for lots of page sketches and layout ideas. *PageMaps* (by Becky Fleck) is another great resource. Also flip through your other magazines for design ideas. Or visit online idea galleries to see what fellow scrappers have created with their photos.

Artwork by Lisa Damrosch

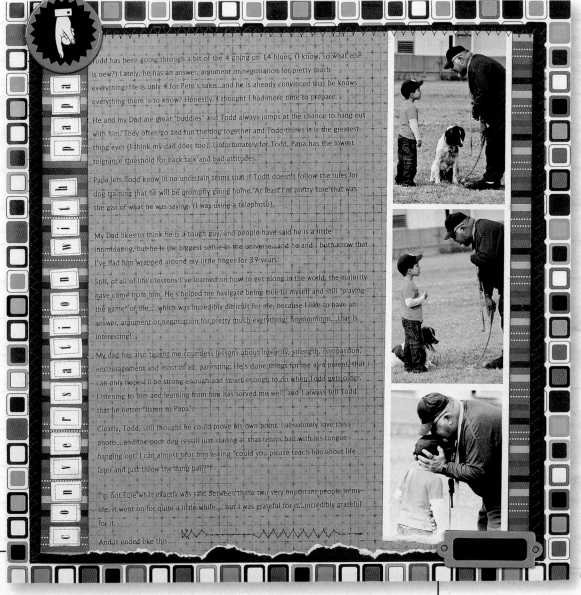

Todd has been going through a bit of the 4 going on 14 blues. (I know, so what else is new?) Lately, he has an answer, argument or negotiation for pretty much everything. He is only 4 for Pete's sake...and he is already convinced that he knows everything there is to know? Honestly, I thought I had more time to prepare.

He and my Dad are great "buddies" and Todd always jumps at the chance to hang out with him. They often go and run the dog together and Todd thinks it is the greatest thing ever (I think my dad does too). Unfortunately for Todd, Papa has the lowest tolerance threshold for back talk and bad attitudes.

Papa lets Todd know in no uncertain terms that if Todd doesn't follow the rules for dog training that he will be promptly going home. At least I'm pretty sure that was the gist of what he was saying. (I was using a telephoto).

My Dad likes to think he is a tough guy, and people have said he is a little intimidating, but he is the biggest softie in the universe...and he and I both know that I've had him wrapped around my little finger for 39 years!

Still, of all of life's lessons I've learned on how to get along in the world, the majority have come from him. He's helped me navigate being true to myself and still "playing the game" of life.... which was incredibly difficult for me, because I like to have an answer, argument or negotiation for pretty much everything! hmmmmmm....that is interesting!

My dad has also taught me countless lessons about integrity, strength, compassion, encouragement and most of all, parenting. He's done things for me as a parent, that I can only hope I'll be strong enough and smart enough to do when Todd gets older. Listening to him and learning from him has served me well, and I always tell Todd that he better "listen to Papa".

Clearly, Todd, still thought he could prove his own point. I absolutely love this photo....and the poor dog is still just staring at that tennis ball with his tongue hanging out! I can almost hear him asking "could you please teach him about life later and just throw the dang ball?"

I'm not sure what exactly was said between these two very important people in my life, it went on for quite a little while..., but I was grateful for it...incredibly grateful for it.

And it ended like this...

Supplies: Cardstock; patterned paper (CherryArte); bookplate (Heidi Swapp); chipboard accent (Scenic Route); Misc: Day Roman font

What a classic moment Lisa captured on this precious layout about her son and his grandpa. Even with the photos taken at such a distance that she couldn't actually hear the conversation, the series of photos were enough to spark her thoughts on the relationship between the two. Even if you don't have the exact words to go along with what is happening in your photos, use your own interpretation as a starting point.

Technique *tip*

To give a series of action photos a storyboard look, resize and arrange in one column using image-editing software. Leave space between each photo to serve as borders. Print the photo strip as one piece.

STARTING POINT

photoboothers

we have a bit of a weakness for those silly photo booths. okay maybe it is just me. but i sure have a couple of willing participants.

city walk
orlando

Jumping in a photo booth for a few fun pictures is a no-brainer for me. I just love the way they capture whoever it is that cares to join me in the booth. This fun photo strip was a result of one such spontaneous shoot. Don't pass up the opportunity to get different kinds of photos taken—it may mean passing up a unique photo starting point for a layout.

STARTING POINT

Supplies: Cardstock; patterned paper (Making Memories, Rusty Pickle); straight pins (Fancy Pants, Heidi Grace); metal brad (Around the Block); stamps (Inkadinkado); Misc: ink

Technique *tip*

If you aren't satisfied with the size or quality of photos taken in places like photo booths, fix them! Scan the photo into your computer and use image-editing software to edit to your liking.

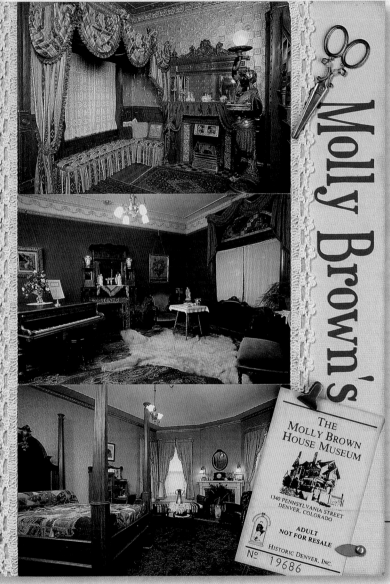

I t is a museum I would have never thought to visit on my own. Honestly, I didn't even know it existed or that it was fairly close to where I lived at the time. But when mom came to visit me in Colorado Springs, it was a site that was top on her list to see. The Molly Brown Museum is located in Denver, which was about an hour north of where I was living. It is the neatest old house which was built in 1890 and was the former residence of the "Unsinkable" Molly Brown. The house was beautiful and interesting and the tour we took was one of the most captivating of stories that I have ever had on a guided tour. It was neat to learn about Molly's life, her famous trip on the Titanic, and her very prominent social life. It was nice to learn about a person and a snippet of history that I never would have otherwise took the time out to do. This visit made me better appreciate the smaller museums that are around when I visit new cities.

Molly Brown's

THE MOLLY BROWN HOUSE MUSEUM

1340 PENNSYLVANIA STREET
DENVER, COLORADO

ADULT
NOT FOR RESALE

HISTORIC DENVER, INC.

N° 19686

STARTING POINT

I didn't think that I would like creating a layout using only postcards from a souvenir shop as visuals. But I was wrong. I really wanted to document a visit to a museum but had no pictures from the experience. These postcards ended up being a great start to a page about that trip. Not only did they provide images I wasn't allowed to take myself, but they also bring back memories that allow me to relive the experience.

Supplies: Cardstock; photo turns (Junkitz); metal clip (Karen Foster); brads (Imaginisce, Making Memories); letter sticker (American Crafts); Misc: Bookman Old Style font, chalk ink, floss, lace

Wait until you read this! ②

Starting your pages with words

Words are a primary starting point for a lot of us who scrapbook. If we didn't have the urge to pair our words with our photos, we would just slip our photos into an album and call it done. But our thoughts and memories do matter to us and that is why words are such an important way in which to begin a layout.

Starting a layout with words doesn't always mean starting with a story. A funny joke, an old journal and a calendar schedule can also be great ways to begin a page. Be inspired to document what you have to say onto your layouts, or to capture what things speak to you. If you keep your mind and ears open to the words around you, you will find many ways in which to start your layouts.

PEANUTS LUNCHTIME COOKBOOK

CHARLES M. SCHULZ

When I realized that I was able to say what I wanted on this layout in just a couple sentences, I let the amount of journaling be the starting point to how the layout's design came together. Instead of putting straight lines of text on the page, I used a combination of letter stickers to give weight to the words and create a photo frame. Be inspired to use something different than the norm to make words on a page stand out.

Something hap pens when you are in the pool. You shine from the Inside Out.

Supplies: Cardstock; letter stickers, patterned paper (Arctic Frog); plastic letters (Heidi Swapp); buttons (Autumn Leaves); rub-ons (Die Cuts With A View); Misc: floss

Technique *tip*

When using letter stickers for journaling, its placement and shape is no longer limited by where a computer will print or materials on which your pen will write. Take advantage of this freedom by experimenting with letter stickers.

STARTING POINT

Something happens when you are in the pool. You shine from the inside out.

He remembers.
Every single one.

Every birthday.
Every anniversary.
Every Valentine's Day.

Every day that is
a chance to show his
wife how much she
is loved...
he remembers.

I love you too, Babe!

always
REMEMBERS.

Since the day my husband and I met, he has been so great about remembering me on special occasions. I have always wanted to document how this makes me feel but never quite knew what to say. Turns out, just a few simple words were all I needed. When documenting something emotionally dear to you, don't let your emotions overwhelm you. Much of the time a few simple phrases are just right.

Supplies: Cardstock; chipboard letters, letter stickers (American Crafts); heart (Heidi Grace); tag (QuicKutz); Misc: Traveling Typewriter font

STARTING
POINT

Technique *tip*

Gift givers all have their own styles of wrapping gifts. Capture them by taking a photo of gifts before they are opened. Then use the photo to inspire some journaling on a page.

Artwork by Kim Moreno

I love pages like this because they really tell a lot about the people they are capturing without extensive journaling to write. Kim cleverly took inventory of the items her son sleeps with. What a cute and insightful memory to look back on. Making an inventory list is a fun and easy way to start a meaningful layout.

Supplies: Cardstock; die-cut shapes, patterned paper (Scenic Route); letter stickers (American Crafts, Scenic Route); chipboard shapes (Deluxe Designs); brads (American Crafts); Misc: ink, ribbon

Technique *tip*

Fun things to take inventory of include purses or wallets, closets, junk drawers, refrigerator, pantry, under the bed, trunk of a car and under couch cushions (eww!).

STARTING POINT

-my blanket
-my body pillow
-your nite-nite
-afghan from the living room
-2 pillows from my bed
-your big Clifford
-Morgan's throw pillow

21 · Benito Juarez' Birthday (M)
Mothering Sunday (UK) · 22
WEEK 13

My son has fallen into the routine of eating the same foods every day. I wanted a fun way to record this, so when I came across this photo of him with his shirt off, I knew I had the perfect solution. Try using photos on a layout as a place to record journaling and integrate your words with your photo.

Supplies: Cardstock; plastic letters (Making Memories); chipboard quotations (American Crafts); Misc: High Tide font, paint

"get in my belly."

– from 'Austin Powers 2' movie

conten
egg sandwich
grapes
orange juice
ham & cheese
veggie chips
water
hot dog
bbq beans

STARTING POINT

egg sandwich
grapes
orange juice
ham + cheese
veggie chips

List
1. lights
2. silk holiday stems
3. sprigs with gold
4. variety of colored balls
5. large gold balls
6. beaded icicles
7. small pinecones
8. decorative ornaments
9. personal ornaments
10. ribbon

Trimmings

I can go years doing the same thing and not take notice of the details, like how I trim our Christmas tree each year. It wasn't until our son started helping that I realized we used the same items each year. I jotted a list during the trimming process, which worked as a simple starting point for this layout.

STARTING POINT

Supplies: Cardstock; patterned paper (Adornit); die-cut letters (QuicKutz); stamps (Inque Boutique); flower (Jo-Ann's); bow accents (Michaels); Misc: glitter, hole punch, ink, markers

List
1. lights
2. silk holiday stems
3. sprigs with gold
4. variety of colored ball
5. large gold balls
6. beaded icicles
7. small pinecones
8. decorat

Technique *tip*

Printing text on a transparency is a great way to fake the look of journaling directly on your background paper. Plus, transparencies add a subtle sheen that makes for more interesting designs.

Looking back on it all,
I can see it so wonderfully.

All of those

Snapshots

in my mind.

The days that have
made up our lives.
The moments that have
filled up our hearts.

The laughter (lots of it).

The memories.

The good stuff in life.

And after all,
that's what it's
really all about.

Those moments that have
been set in our paths.

Those memories that
sing in our souls.

Those things that
remind us of just
how lucky we are.

It really is a

Beautiful

thing.

Supplies: Cardstock (Bazzill); patterned paper (American Crafts, Scenic Route); overlay (Creative Imaginations); photo corners (American Crafts); buttons (Autumn Leaves)

How refreshing it is to just sit down and write a few beautiful words to your family. So many times our journaling is about one particular family member, a single event or a solitary memory. Don't forget the big picture when sharing your thoughts on your pages, and in doing so you may just create the perfect intro page for your next family album.

STARTING POINT

*The memories.
The good stuff of life.*

*And afterall,
that's what it's
really all about.*

When we travel, we experience more than just the beauty and sights of a new place. So, words that go beyond "just the facts" are a great starting point for your vacation layouts. For this page about a trip to Europe, I wanted to document more than just the things we saw, so I journaled about what the trip meant to me.

Supplies: Cardstock; chipboard frame, letter stickers, patterned paper (Dream Street); chipboard accents (BasicGrey); buttons (Autumn Leaves); fabric words (Jo-Ann's); Misc: ink, paint

Technique *tip*

Bring along a journal when you travel. Take downtime on the airplane or in the hotel to jot down your thoughts.

STARTING POINT

If I would've known what a kick you would get out of hearing it, I would've said it a long time ago. The first time I said the word 'shush', it stopped you right in your tracks and made you laugh harder than I had heard you laugh in awhile. You proceeded to repeat the word, adding a little more 'juice' to it, and laughing harder each time you did. It has now become a word without meaning, except to provide one extensive giggle session. [06/07]

SHUSH,

All I have to do is read the title of this layout and I find myself laughing, which is exactly the reason I just had to use it. This one word cracks up my son more than any other—I guess the sound of it just strikes him as funny—so it was a great topic for a fun layout. Use words or phrases that your family often says as inspiration for a layout title.

Supplies: Cardstock (Bazzill); patterned paper, ribbon (SEI); letter stickers (American Crafts); paperclip (Magic Scraps); brad (Karen Foster); Misc: Traveling Typewriter font

"Shush"

STARTING POINT

Technique *tip*

Tape-record a family dinner or set up the camcorder one afternoon. You'll get lots of choice quotes to use on pages.

Technique *tip*

Using a playful font, as Kelly did here, lends the perfect childlike touch to pages about those funny things kids say.

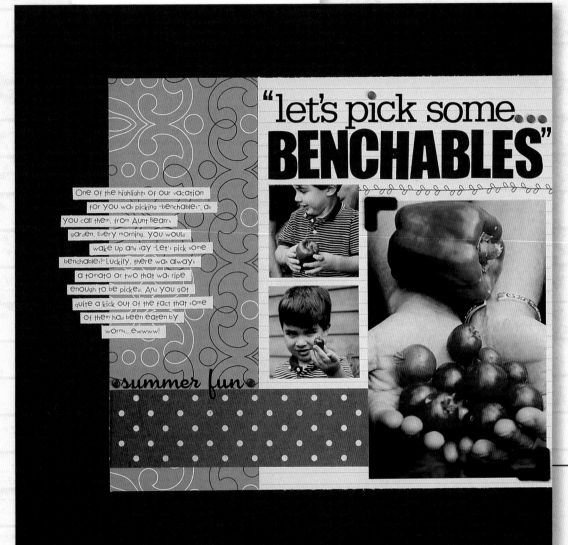

"let's pick some...
BENCHABLES"

One of the highlights of our vacation for you was picking "benchables", as you call them, from Aunt Bean's garden. Every morning, you would wake up and say "Let's pick some benchables!" Luckily, there was always a tomato or two that was ripe enough to be picked. And you got quite a kick out of the fact that some of them had been eaten by worms...ewwww!

summer fun

Artwork by Kelly Noel

Supplies: Cardstock (Bazzill); patterned paper, stickers (American Crafts, Scenic Route); brads, rub-ons (American Crafts); Misc: 2Peas Favorite Things font

Kelly lets her son's own words be the guide for this super cute page about picking "benchables." By using the exact words of her son, she adds her son's voice and personality to her page. Starting a layout with the words of a loved one makes for precious and authentic pages, and gets your own words flowing.

"Let's pick some benchables."

STARTING POINT

This is one layout idea that I would never get tired of seeing. Not only does it look like Amy had a great time creating this layout, but I can just hear the giggles and voices as each of her children gave their answers. Involve your family in the journaling on your layouts and keep their voices alive.

Artwork by Amy Licht

Supplies: Cardstock; patterned paper (BoBunny, Prima); chipboard letters (Chatterbox); chipboard symbols (BasicGrey, Heidi Swapp); fabric tabs (Scrapworks); decorative tape (Imagination Project); photo corners (Canson); flower and heart accents (Making Memories); brads (Bazzill, Making Memories); Misc: Tubby font, floss, paint

Technique *tip*

To really make quotes or conversations come to life on a page, pair them with photos that show a bit of personality. Photos with gestures, hugs or quirky grins will enhance the character of your subject much more than perfectly posed portraits.

Who eats the most?
J: Me
A: Me
S: Abby (that girl can eat)

STARTING POINT

Artwork by Lisa Damrosch

STARTING POINT

"Mom, I just want to kiss G, but I want to kiss her when my friends aren't around but I have too many friends and they are always around."

Conversations are priceless snippets of life between us and the people around us. They become especially entertaining when they involve a little one. Lisa brought the voice of her son alive by starting her page with a word-for-word conversation she had with him. Bring your family's voices—young or old—onto your layouts by recording conversations for inspiration.

Supplies: Patterned paper (Creative Imaginations, Me & My Big Ideas); chipboard hearts and letters (Heidi Swapp); rub-ons (KI Memories)

Supplies: Cardstock; patterned paper (A2Z); letter stickers (American Crafts); wiggle eyes (Chenille Kraft); Misc: Quirky font, floss

I adore the time when kids start to form a sense of humor. It's even more fun when they get the idea of a joke and learn to tell a few themselves. So it was only natural that I create a layout to commemorate the first joke my son fell in love with telling. Along with first words, use first jokes and another first sayings as starting points for your child's pages.

How to Say it

Don't let your message get lost on a page. Remember these guidelines when journaling:

• Text is easier to read in small amounts. Try adding short captions around a layout. Or put lots of text in a narrow column so it's not as overwhelming.

• Match the mood or emotion of your words to their style. Consider the font, whether the words are handwritten or typed, the color, the shape of the journaling box and the size of the text.

• Whether you handwrite or type your journaling, make sure the text is readable. If the text is small, write neatly or use a san serif font. Or make text larger if you use a messier style.

STARTING POINT

"Knock knock."
"Who's there?"
"Banana"
"Banana who?"

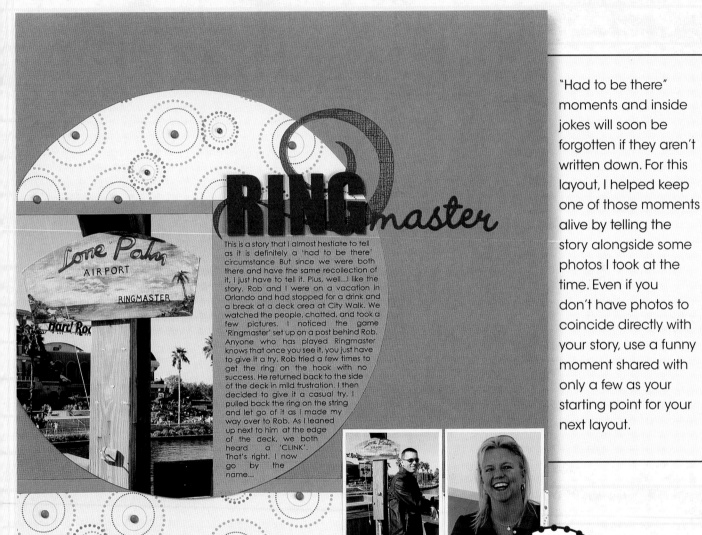

RING *master*

This is a story that I almost hesitate to tell as it is definitely a 'had to be there' circumstance But since we were both there and have the same recollection of it, I just have to tell it. Plus, well...I like the story. Rob and I were on a vacation in Orlando and had stopped for a drink and a break at a deck area at City Walk. We watched the people, chatted, and took a few pictures. I noticed the game 'Ringmaster' set up on a post behind Rob. Anyone who has played Ringmaster knows that once you see it, you just have to give it a try. Rob tried a few times to get the ring on the hook with no success. He returned back to the side of the deck in mild frustration. I then decided to give it a casual try. I pulled back the ring on the string and let go of it as I made my way over to Rob. As I leaned up next to him at the edge of the deck, we both heard a 'CLINK'. That's right. I now go by the name...

"Had to be there" moments and inside jokes will soon be forgotten if they aren't written down. For this layout, I helped keep one of those moments alive by telling the story alongside some photos I took at the time. Even if you don't have photos to coincide directly with your story, use a funny moment shared with only a few as your starting point for your next layout.

Supplies: Cardstock (Bazzill); patterned paper (Scenic Route); letter stickers (American Crafts); die-cut letters (QuicKutz); brads (Queen & Co.); stamp (Inque Boutique); Misc: Century Gothic font

Technique *tip*

Use symbolism to mimic the theme on your layouts. Here, I played off the ring theme by including papers with circles and used other round elements.

STARTING POINT

This is a story that I almost hesitate to tell as it is definitely a "had to be there" circumstance.

Technique *tip*

When including more than one person's words on a layout, type one and handwrite the other to keep them separate.

Artwork by Summer Fullerton

tooth(less)

MONDAY
APRIL 2 2007

Dear Tooth Fairy,
I lost my tooth on the play-ground and I couldn't find it
me
Love
corinne

The secretary from the school called this afternoon explaining you had been hit in the face at recess and had come to the nurses office bleeding. After a second look it turned out the bleeding was the result of a missing tooth. The tooth was nowhere to be found and you were heartbroken.

When you arrived home we decided a note to the tooth fairy would be a great solution to our missing tooth problem. That night you carefully placed the note and your tooth fairy box next to your bed with hopes she would still come for a visit later that evening.

Two days later the secretary called again. The conversation that followed is still a bit unbelievable. Someone had found a tooth on the playground and returned it to the office. The secretary and I had a good giggle and we both agreed the tooth had to belong to you.

I love it when kids' words make it onto layouts, but I love it even more when their handwriting does too. Summer does a fabulous job of combining both her and her daughter's words on this layout by including an actual letter written by her daughter summarizing her own account of the event. Pair your subject's handwriting with their photos to start a truly personalized layout.

Dear Tooth Fairy,
I lost my tooth on the play-ground and I couldn't find it
me
Love
corinne

STARTING POINT

Supplies: Cardstock; patterned paper (Scenic Route); chipboard letters (American Crafts, Scenic Route); felt flowers (American Crafts); paper flowers (Savvy Stamps); rub-ons (Heidi Grace); day sticker (Heidi Swapp); brads (Queen & Co.); heart accents (Making Memories); Misc: AvantGarde font

Some notes and gestures are just too touching to be kept in a box. These calendar pages that my husband brought home from work are great examples. I love the sentiments that he took time to share and just had to return the gesture by keeping them alive on a layout. Keep quotations and notes alive on a layout by using them as a starting point on your next page.

Rob is admittedly not the most cup-half-full person. It's not that he's negative, because he is far from a 'downer'. But he does like to at least consider the sometimes 'not so pleasant' alternative situation. He feels it is his job to make sure he prepares for and acknowledges all possible situations, even if they may be unpleasant.

Because of this, I try and infiltrate him with as much of my optimism and positive-thinking as possible. One tiny way I do this is by stuffing his stocking each year with a one-a-day calendar just filled with motivation and things to think about (that aren't negative). For all I knew, this calendar made it to work with him, but didn't do much more than tell him what date it was. I wasn't sure if he was reading the daily insights, let alone letting them soak in.

That was until October 15.

Rob had left for work early one morning before anyone else was awake. When I got up and went into the kitchen, I found this October 14 page from his calendar on the counter for me to see. It meant the word to me. Not just because of what it said, but because of who it came from. Not only was my husband reading the calendar, but he was sharing a positive message with ME. It melted my heart.

One more message followed that year. It's no surprise that I kept both as they meant more to me than he will know. Most of all because they came from him.

2007

HELLO my name is THE messenger

Start the day with love, live the day with love, end the day with love.

SUNDAY OCTOBER 14

A powerful exercise to practice on a regular basis is to imagine that this is your final goodbye. Imagine that, for some reason or another, you won't see your family ever again after this meeting. Would you remind your parent, child, sibling, spouse, or other loved one of yet another shortcoming, flaw, or imperfection? Would your last words be complaints or pessimistic comments that suggest that you wish your life were different than it is? Probably not.

SATURDAY DECEMBER 1

Supplies: Cardstock; patterned paper (American Crafts, Chatterbox); rub-ons (Maya Road); buttons (Jo-Ann's); die-cut tag (QuicKutz); Misc: Impact font, floss

Technique *tip*

Love saving memorabilia but afraid of being buried by it all? Save all clippings, notes, tickets, etc. for a year in a box. At the end of the year, go through and only keep those things that still really speak to you.

STARTING POINT

Start the day with love, live the day with love, end the day with love.

SUNDAY OCTOBER 14

Artwork by Denine Zielinski

Everyone has a song that strikes a chord (pun intended). On this charming layout about her son, Denine let a verse from a Barry White song be the starting point to complete a meaningful page with heartfelt journaling. If you have a song verse that you love, use those words as inspiration.

Supplies: Cardstock; patterned paper (BoBunny, KI Memories); letter stickers, paper frills (Doodlebug); chipboard shapes (Scenic Route); brads (Stemma); stamps (Fontwerks); ribbon (May Arts); metal clip (Making Memories); accent stickers (Scenic Route, Stampin' Up); Misc: BlackJack and Old Remington fonts, circle punches

My First, My Last, My Everything
By Barry White

My first, my last, my everything.
And the answer to all my dreams.
You're my sun, my moon,
my guiding star.
My kind of wonderful,
that's what you are.

STARTING POINT

Technique *tip*

Whether you've run out of thread, don't know how to sew or want to avoid the texture, you can fake the look of stitching on your page. Use a straight edge and pencil to mark dots about every 3/16". Then use a paper piercer to punch holes where the dots are. Then draw a line through the holes with a pen.

Supplies: Cardstock; letter stickers (American Crafts); flowers (Making Memories); fabric brads (Karen Foster); paper frills (Doodlebug); Misc: SP Sara Jean font

Every time I look at this purse I can't help but think how appreciative I am of my dad. I read my dad's note, took a picture of the purse and allowed myself to journal the feelings that come to me when I use this gift. Think about someone or something you appreciate and be inspired to extend your thanks onto a page.

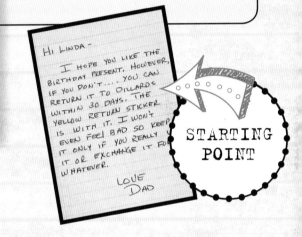

Hi Linda—
I hope you like the birthday present. However, if you don't..... you can return it to Dillards within 30 days. The yellow return sticker is with it. I won't even feel bad so keep it only if you really want it or exchange it for whatever.

LOVE
DAD

STARTING POINT

My husband and I wrote some thoughts on how we feel about each other, which I used as my starting point for this layout. Getting Rob's words on my layouts, especially in his handwriting, is something I will cherish. What better inspiration for a loving page than to start with loving words?

These are our thoughts about how we met and how we knew each other was the one, written in each of our own handwriting and in our own words. We never want to forget how we feel about how our lives were meant to be spent together.　(Written: 2005　Layout: 2008)

WRITTEN BY ROB

meant to·bes

ALWAYS & FOREVER

STARTING POINT

Supplies: Cardstock; patterned paper (Jenni Bowlin); chipboard letters (Heidi Swapp); denim pocket, letter stickers (Making Memories); chipboard accent, metal heart (Creative Imaginations); photo turn (7gypsies); Misc: Arial font

To my wife in my words:
I am very happy that we found each other at the time that we did. I feel it couldn't have been any better timing for either of us. I needed you. You have filled my life with love and happiness. You are the world's best wife to me and mom to Robby. I couldn't imagine being any happier than I am right and I look forward to many wonderful years together.
Love Always,
Rob

As written by me, in my 5th grade English journal - 1981

If I had to advertise myself

I have blonde hair and blue eyes. I don't have any freckles. My personality is sometimes nice and sometimes mad. Most of the time its nice. I like a lot of little things julery and sparts I don't really like fancy stuff. Espessially fancy clothes. That's the main thing.

it would be

IN A MAGAZINE

I recently came across my fifth-grade English journal. Inside was a fascinating look into how I thought, how I wrote, and what was on my mind at that time. This particular entry struck me as a great starting point for a layout about my former self. If you have saved writing from when you were younger, pair them with photos of you from that same age for a great old-school memory page.

Supplies: Cardstock; patterned paper (Paper Wishes); chipboard letters (Heidi Swapp); chipboard shapes (Fancy Pants); metal clip (Making Memories); letter stamps (Inque Boutique); Misc: Century Gothic, Minya Nouvelle and Segoe Print fonts, ink, paint

STARTING POINT

Sometime after I was married, mom gave me some old paperwork and memorabilia from when I was a child. One of my most absolute favorite pieces is a booklet given to mom and dad at the hospital after I was born. It is a small pamphlet that tells how to take care of their new baby. It is so interesting to read the advice as given decades ago and how it differs from today. However, that isn't my favorite part of the book. On the back, in mom's handwriting, is a list of potential names that she and dad had chosen for me. The list reads like this:

Jennifer Lynn

Ginger Renee

Linda Marie

Michele

Sheri Lyn

Cindy

Kathy

I'm not sure how long it took them to decide on my name, or why they decided on the third one on their list, but I do know that according to that same booklet, I officially left the hospital temporarily being known as, *Sweetie Pie.*

sweetie pie

Supplies: Cardstock; flowers (Doodlebug, Making Memories); brads (Making Memories); Misc: Rockwell and Segoe Script fonts, corner rounder, paper clip

I am so grateful to have the information contained on this layout, and it's such a fun story to tell. The actual memorabilia that contains this text is too valuable to put on a layout, but I was happy to include just the meaningful text and keep the actual document in a safe place. Go through your most valuable paper possessions for inspiration of words you may want to document on your scrapbook pages.

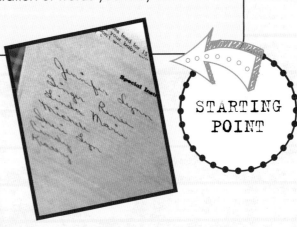

STARTING POINT

Technique *tip*

Ask various family members for any significant documents and memorabilia they have. Scan the papers into your computer for scrapping later on.

Growth Analysis

2001: 6 lbs. 10 oz., 21"

2002: 20 lbs. 7 oz., 31"

2003: 23 lbs., 33"

2004: 29 lbs., 37"

2005: 32 lbs., 39"

2006: 34 lbs., 40"

2007: 37 lbs., 43"

Scarlett experienced rapid growth during her first year, followed by a steady five-year increase. Continued growth is expected.

0　1　2　3　4　5　6

Artwork by Lisa Moorefield

Is there a more fitting way to show the growth of a child than with a growth chart? Here, words weren't the inspiration for the layout's theme, but words did provide the beginning for the page. Lisa let a simple graph inspire her to write a few fun words, creating a playful, informative page. Think outside the (journaling) box for creative layout starting points.

Supplies: Cardstock; patterned paper (Making Memories); letter stickers (American Crafts); Misc: American Typewriter font

Technique *tip*

Growth isn't the only information you could display in chart form. Try creating a layout about your family's activities. For example, make a pie chart showing how much time in a week your family spends on certain activities like watching TV, going to work or school, playing sports or doing religious activities.

STARTING POINT

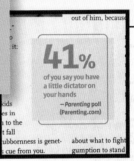

Got Spunk?

41% of you say you have a little dictator on your hands. *-Parenting* poll

I would have to say that our Miss Emily falls right smack in the middle of that forty-one percent. Okay, maybe dictator is a bit on the harsh side. I might lean a little more toward master, boss, or ruler in Emily's case. She is quite feisty and sure does know how to get exactly what she wants. In most cases, it is either her way or the highway. You'll do just fine as long as you comply. It's simply a part of who she is, and we all love her just the same. She wouldn't be our little Miss Emily if she didn't have that special brand of spunk. So, what's wrong with a little tyranny in the family? After all, somebody has to be the boss.

Artwork by Denine Zielinski

I'm intrigued by the random statistics in magazines. On this layout, Denine did a wonderful job of letting such a statistic lead the way for her layout about her niece. When flipping through your favorite magazines, keep your eyes open for ideas that catch your eye. You never know what will inspire your journaling.

Supplies: Cardstock; patterned paper (A2Z, Imaginisce); letter stickers (Arctic Frog, Doodlebug); plastic flowers (American Crafts); buttons (My Mind's Eye); brads (Boxer Scrapbook); dimensional paint (Duncan); Misc: Times New Roman

STARTING POINT

41% of you say you have a little dictator on your hands
—*Parenting* poll (Parenting.com)

My son fell in love with Charlie Brown after watching his first season of Charlie Brown holiday specials on TV. And I can't blame him; Charlie Brown was a childhood favorite of mine as well. Being fans, we acquired this cute book that contains timeless Peanuts cartoons. I used one cartoon as a fun way to add to the journaling on this layout about my family and their donuts. Look to comics or other books for a great way to enhance a layout with words.

Supplies: Cardstock; patterned paper (Fancy Pants, My Mind's Eye); wood frame (Chatterbox); stamps (Inque Boutique); ribbon (BoBunny); ribbon slide (Making Memories); rub-on stitches (K&Co.); Misc: Teen font

STARTING POINT

SMALL GESTURES **big** REWARDS

STARTING POINT

As you go through life, you will come across some words of advice that are said so often and with such casualness that you may even become immune to what the words are actually saying. It will happen.

However there is one simple statement that relates to how to treat people that I think is worth reiterating. I want you to realize what an impact living by the words of one statement can affect your life, your character and the lives of those you love.

" No act of kindness, no matter how small, is ever wasted." *Aesop*

In a period of childhood where you are socially excused for being self-centered or unsympathetic, you are neither. You are already so mindful of those around you; how they feel and what you can do to make them laugh or make them happy. You use your manners more than can be expected of a little guy and you pout if you see hugs being given that you are not a part of. I love that you are already in touch with what being kind means to those around you and I think you already see and feel the benefits it gives you in return. My hope is that you keep that with you as you grow. I hope that no amount of negative situations or people ever penetrate that natural desire within you to be kind. I love you little guy and thank you for already make my life a much happier place thanks to your kindness and your affections. You are one special little man.

In contrast to those times that I am at a loss for words, there are times when I'm able to journal with an overabundance of words. In order to better channel my thoughts on this layout, I found a quote, which worked perfectly to focus my journaling into a cohesive thought. Use quotes to jump-start your thoughts whether your words are many or few.

Supplies: Cardstock; flowers, patterned paper, plastic letters (Making Memories); Misc: Times New Roman font

How to *Say* it

When you start your page with words, you probably want them to be the focus. Try these tips for making words stand out:

• If you use bold or abundant embellishments, make your words even bolder.

• Draw extra attention to words with die-cut arrows, chipboard quotations or large brackets.

• Highlight key words using letters stickers or different fonts.

• Use a bold journaling block to enhance plain or handwritten words.

I've started taking photos of things that I like but really don't need anymore. It's a way to keep the memories alive without having the actual object cluttering my space. These photos prove handy when I am inspired to create a layout about the story behind, or my memories of, a particular item. Keep the clutter out of your home and the memories in your albums by writing about those items that you no longer have, but that held a special little place in your heart.

Supplies: Cardstock; metal clip, patterned paper, photo anchor (Making Memories); letter stamps (Inque Boutique); chipboard letter (Heidi Swapp); ribbon (Offray); flowers (Doodlebug); Misc: Traveling Typewriter font, ink

STARTING POINT

I just have to let you know what a great souvenir I had once chosen for you.

Technique *tip*

Before your next yard sale or trip to Goodwill, get out your camera and snap a few photos of the items you are about to part with. Use them to journal about the individual items or about the donation itself.

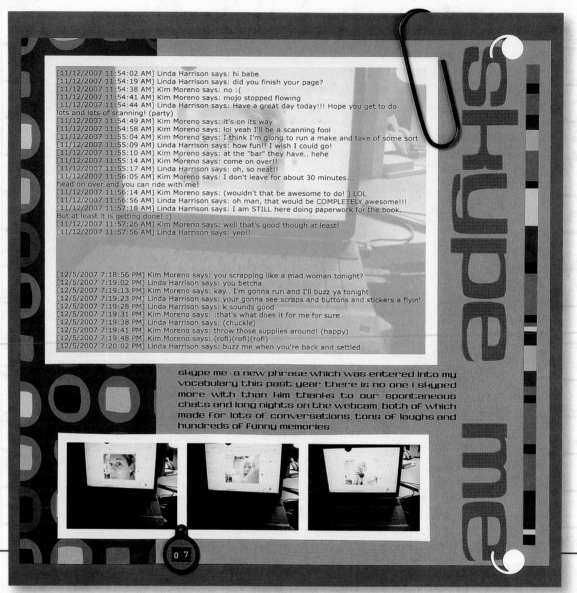

[11/12/2007 11:54:02 AM] Linda Harrison says: hi babe
[11/12/2007 11:54:19 AM] Linda Harrison says: did you finish your page?
[11/12/2007 11:54:38 AM] Kim Moreno says: no :(
[11/12/2007 11:54:41 AM] Kim Moreno says: mojo stopped flowing
[11/12/2007 11:54:44 AM] Linda Harrison says: Have a great day today!!! Hope you get to do lots and lots of scanning! (party)
[11/12/2007 11:54:49 AM] Kim Moreno says: it's on its way
[11/12/2007 11:54:58 AM] Kim Moreno says: lol yeah I'll be a scanning fool
[11/12/2007 11:55:04 AM] Kim Moreno says: I think I'm going to run a make and take of some sort
[11/12/2007 11:55:09 AM] Linda Harrison says: how fun!! I wish I could go!
[11/12/2007 11:55:10 AM] Kim Moreno says: at the "bar" they have.. hehe
[11/12/2007 11:55:14 AM] Kim Moreno says: come on over!!
[11/12/2007 11:55:17 AM] Linda Harrison says: oh, so neat!!
[11/12/2007 11:56:05 AM] Kim Moreno says: I don't leave for about 30 minutes... head on over and you can ride with me!
[11/12/2007 11:56:14 AM] Kim Moreno says: (wouldn't that be awesome to do!) LOL
[11/12/2007 11:56:56 AM] Linda Harrison says: oh man, that would be COMPLETELY awesome!!!
[11/12/2007 11:57:18 AM] Linda Harrison says: I am STILL here doing paperwork for the book. But at least it is getting done! :)
[11/12/2007 11:57:26 AM] Kim Moreno says: well that's good though at least!
[11/12/2007 11:57:56 AM] Linda Harrison says: yep!!

[12/5/2007 7:18:56 PM] Kim Moreno says: you scrapping like a mad woman tonight?
[12/5/2007 7:19:02 PM] Linda Harrison says: you betcha
[12/5/2007 7:19:13 PM] Kim Moreno says: kay.. I'm gonna run and I'll buzz you tonight
[12/5/2007 7:19:23 PM] Linda Harrison says: your gonna see scraps and buttons and stickers a flyin'
[12/5/2007 7:19:28 PM] Linda Harrison says: k sounds good
[12/5/2007 7:19:31 PM] Kim Moreno says: :that's what does it for me for sure
[12/5/2007 7:19:38 PM] Linda Harrison says: (chuckle)
[12/5/2007 7:19:41 PM] Kim Moreno says: throw those supplies around! (happy)
[12/5/2007 7:19:48 PM] Kim Moreno says: (rofl)(rofl)(rofl)
[12/5/2007 7:20:02 PM] Linda Harrison says: buzz me when you're back and settled

skype me -a new phrase which was entered into my vocabulary this past year there is no one i skyped more with than kim thanks to our spontaneous chats and long nights on the webcam, both of which made for lots of conversations, tons of laughs and hundreds of funny memories.

skype me

Skype has changed the atmosphere of my evenings spent scrapping. Now, instead of doing so alone, I am joined virtually by one of a number of friends. Most nights it's my friend Kim, so it was only natural that I take clips of some of our many conversations and use them as a starting point for this layout. When I look at things we wrote even a week ago, I start laughing, and I can imagine how priceless these kept conversations will be years from now.

Supplies: Cardstock; patterned paper (Tinkering Ink); large paper clip (Bazzill); metal tag (7gypsies); number stickers (Making Memories); die-cut quotes (QuicKutz); Misc: Pine Lint Germ font

STARTING POINT

Technique *tip*

Create folders on your computer labeled with those you chat with most online. Periodically, save a conversation into a folder for instant starting points.

[12/5/2007 7:18:56 PM] Kim Moreno says: you scrapping like a mad woman tonight?
[12/5/2007 7:19:02 PM] Linda Harrison says: you betcha
[12/5/2007 7:19:13 PM] Kim Moreno says: kay...I'm gonna run and I'll buzz ya tonight

Technique *tip*

When creating a list of new resolutions, do it on a layout! "Breaking up" with bad habits on a page will leave you a little more account-able than if you don't scrap about it them all.

It wouldn't be fair to place all the blame on you, but you have to admit that you did contribute to my addition of a few extra pounds this past year. You are always ready and always quick and you tempt me by being available any time I was in need. Well, this year I am not giving into the lure of your convenience. I will not do it. And to tell you the truth, I never really liked you all that much in the first place. You were just a bad habit bound to be broken. You and I don't have a future together and that's just the way it is. Goodbye.

Most of us have something in our lives that we want to limit or quit entirely. A fun way to document your desire to limit something in your life is to scrap it! Here I wrote a breakup letter to McDonald's and its lure of convenience when I'm out and about. Use your desire to change something in your life as a fun start to a layout.

Supplies: Cardstock; patterned paper (Tinkering Ink); chipboard letters (Heidi Swapp); letter stickers (American Crafts); photo turns (7gypsies); chipboard icon (Scenic Route); brads (Making Memories); rub-ons (Fontwerks); Misc: Incognitype font

2008 Resolutions
1. Stop eating at McDonald's!

STARTING POINT

unusual

unsurpassed

unprecedented

unforgettable

unexpected

unique

one of a kind

Don't you just love it?

③

Starting your pages with product

You probably intend to start your pages with photos or stories. But embellishments, pretty stationery, colorful party supplies, even clothing tags, are sometimes too irresistible; you have to get them on a layout! Some of the best layouts come out of our desire to just play with pretty and inspiring product. That's okay! You can start a layout just for the sake of using product and still create a meaningful page. In this chapter, scrapbook supplies, craft materials, note cards and other types of products illustrate how to successfully begin a layout with a product you want to use on it.

EXPECT THE
Unexpected

Completely casual fabulously fun, and contagiously cute! That's what you two are. You make every day we spend out together such a fun time and every day we spend at home such a joy. When I am with you both I am at my best. I feel I am right where I am meant to be. With you two, I am happy, content and most likely laughing too. You both make the tough parts of life easier and the happy parts happier. You make me smile on the inside even if I may not be on the outside. I love you guys with everything I got and thank you both for the love you give to me.

For this layout, I finally got to use product I had ignored for a while. I started with a sheet of patterned paper and went through all my supplies on a hunt to collect what coordinated with the paper. In the end, I found a desk full of products that I would have never used if I hadn't started with the paper. "Shop" around your supply stash when looking for a great starting point.

Supplies: Cardstock; patterned paper (BoBunny); acrylic letters (Heidi Swapp); chipboard shapes (KI Memories, Provo Craft); denim pocket (Making Memories); heart shape, pins (Heidi Grace); ribbon (SEI); Misc: Arial font, floss

Technique *tip*

Pick out a random sample of products from your stash and challenge yourself to use them together on a layout.

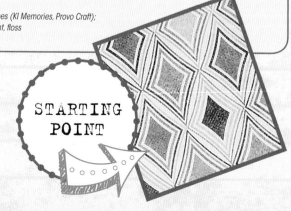

STARTING POINT

When I came across this graphic patterned paper, what stood out to me was not the cool geometric design but the tiny black Xs, which immediately reminded me of cross-stitching. I love adding stitches to layouts, so this was a great opportunity to add tons of hand stitching to mimic the patterned paper. The next time you're looking through your stash of paper, look for ways the designs can be inspiration for adding your favorite touches to a layout.

Supplies: Cardstock; patterned paper, sticker accents (Tinkering Ink); bookplate, chipboard letters (Heidi Swapp); brads, metal-rimmed frames (Making Memories); buttons (Jo-Ann's); Misc: circle punches, floss

STARTING POINT

How to *Use* it

Starting your page with product doesn't just mean you have to use it as a part of the page. It can become the start of the page. Here are some ideas to make your products shine:

• Cut out a large pattern from paper and use that as the image on your layout.

• Gather several words embellishments and write a poem with them.

• Use acrylic paint to create a masterpiece on a page.

• Use brads to create a polka dot background.

• Add clear dimensional adhesive or iridescent medium to paper and chipboard embellishments.

When going to scrapbook these photos of my son with his fake bug collection, I couldn't help but be inspired by some adorable products featuring bugs and bright colors. I try to stay away from anything too cutesy on my layouts so that I keep them timeless, but no one can resist cute all the time. Using fun, adorable products to accompany your photos is a fun way to start a kid-friendly layout.

Supplies: Cardstock (Bazzill); patterned paper, rub-ons (Karen Foster); letter stickers (American Crafts); die-cut circles (QuicKutz); buttons (Jo-Ann's); Misc: Love Ya Like a Sister font, floss

STARTING POINT

Technique *tip*

If you're inspired by patterned paper but don't have any matching embellishments, make your own! Simply cut out parts of the paper design and attach the pieces to your layout with adhesive foam.

I was quite surprised when I arrived to pick you up from Grammo's house one day and found you doing this. Although you had been out of the toddler swings for quite some time, you definitely weren't completely confident on the bigger swings yet. However, after this particular day spent at Grammo's, it looked as if that had changed, and there you were, growing up right in front of me once again. 05.2007

I love using buttons. But on this layout, I strayed from my usual way of grouping them and let the design on a sheet of patterned paper be the starting point. By following a pattern that was already in place, my buttons took on a unique arrangement that alone I would not have considered.

Supplies: Cardstock; patterned paper (Making Memories) buttons (Jo-Ann's); die-cut arrow (QuickKutz); Misc: Times New Roman font, circle punch

STARTING POINT

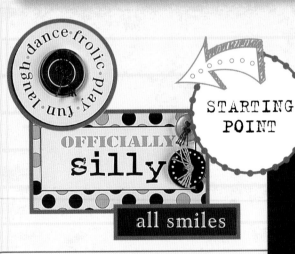

STARTING POINT

Sheets of matching embellishments are always fun to look at. But when I use one piece here and there on different layouts, the collection's effect gets lost. I decided to let an entire sheet of embellishments be my starting point for this energetic page. By using pieces from the same collection on one page, I kept the impact of the product alive.

Supplies: Cardstock; chipboard shapes (Scenic Route); stamps (Sassafras Lass); buttons (Jo-Ann's); Misc: floss, ink

Artwork by Lisa Moorefield

friends

- play together
- argue sometimes
- snuggle and hug
- help each other
- cry if separated
- care and love

forever friends

STARTING POINT

create

More is not always better. This holds true when starting a page with a particular embellishment that you want to make the focus. On this layout, Lisa started with a metal sentiment embellishment and used that one embellishment to dictate the rest of her layout. If you want what you put on your page to be noticed, be inspired to use the "less-is-more" philosophy.

Supplies: Cardstock; patterned paper (MOD); chipboard letters (BasicGrey, Heidi Swapp, Making Memories, Queen & Co.); flower (Prima); brads, metal word, ribbon (Making Memories); Misc: SP Coffee Break font, thread

Technique *tip*

With their understated size, singular sentiments are great starting points for small pages. Also try using them as starting points for a mini album.

Leah's birthday party

Turning

FIVE

Random snapshots from

Supplies: Cardstock; letter stickers (American Crafts); square punch (EK Success); gift accent (KI Memories)

There are some embellishments that are so adorable you can't help but want to amplify their cuteness. That is what I did with the sweet little embellishment that inspired this page about my niece's birthday. I used the one embellishment as a bright beginning for the entire design of the layout. With so many fun embellishments available, you're bound to find one that's the perfect starting point for a lively design.

STARTING POINT

Technique *tip*

Don't overlook even small embellishments as a source for design or color inspiration. Copy the patterns on fabric brads, look at color combinations in packs of ribbon or check out the shapes and textures on sticker sheets.

Technique *tip*

To save time, create your own product "collections." Go through your stash of supplies and gather groups of product—patterned paper, cardstock, embellishments—that coordinate. Pack groups in individual bags to use later on a page.

Artwork by Kelly Noel

So many manufacturers do a fantastic job of creating product collections with endless possibilities. For this layout, Kelly used products from one line to create a festively unified page about her son's birthday. Starting a layout with a line of coordinating product isn't just a quick way to get started, it also makes for foolproof page designs with tons of personality.

Supplies: Cardstock; chipboard shapes, letter stickers, patterned paper, ribbon, rub-ons (American Crafts)

STARTING POINT

I'm so grateful for coming across this sticker sheet with a cooking theme. Without this as an inspiration, I would not have thought to make a layout about the times my son and I spend in the kitchen together. When I saw these cute stickers, I knew it was the perfect kick I needed to get out the camera and capture one of these special times. Let themed products be a starting point for layouts you may have neglected to record.

Supplies: Cardstock; patterned paper (Arctic Frog); chipboard letters (Heidi Swapp); sticker accents (Flair); photo turns (Junkitz); Misc: Book Antiqua font

Technique *tip*

When using a sheet of stickers, remember that you don't have to use the whole sheet! A few well-placed elements will highlight a page's theme just as effectively as lots of embellishment.

STARTING POINT

Artwork by Denine Zielinski

Just when I think I've looked at a particular product from every angle, I come across a fresh idea. Denine's flawless combination of metal-rimmed tags, hand stitching, colored paper and buttons show that there is always another way to use products you have used many times before. Use a combination of your favorite products to inspire you to create unique embellishments you wouldn't have created by using each product on its own.

Supplies: Cardstock; patterned paper (BasicGrey, Daisy D's, Deja Views); rub-ons (Creative Imaginations, Heidi Grace); buttons (BasicGrey, My Mind's Eye); stamps (Limited Edition); metal-rimmed tags (Making Memories); die-cut shapes (Sizzix); Misc: Bernhart, Fling and Prissy Frat fonts, circle punches, floss, ink

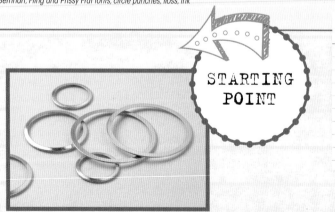

STARTING POINT

Technique *tip*

Push your products and imagination to the edge. Gather some of your favorite products and brainstorm about all the ways in which you can use them on your pages.

Artwork by Amy Licht

I don't think a title could be any more bold or fun! Amy shows how a collection of one kind of embellishment can be a great starting point for an interesting layout. Here, Amy put a variety of metal rimmed tags to use as a title for her refreshing summer page. If the opposite of less is more was ever true, this is a fantastic example.

Supplies: Cardstock; patterned paper (American Crafts, Arctic Frog, Autumn Leaves, Doodlebug, Imagination Project, K&Co., KI Memories, Scenic Route, SEI); metal-rimmed tags (Avery, Jo-Ann's); brads, letter stickers (Making Memories); rub-ons (American Crafts); Misc: Love Letter font, corner rounder

Technique tip

Grouping multiple embellishments, rather than spreading them around the page, will keep a layout's design more simplified.

STARTING POINT

Artwork by Kim Moreno

I really like the look and feel of texture added to a scrapbook page. There are plenty of ways to achieve this look, but one really cool and classy way to do so is by using dry embossing. Inspired by the look of the plates for her embossing tool, Kim created a page about the zoo, adding perfectly placed texture to match her page's theme. Let the patterns on your tools spark ideas for your next layout.

Supplies: Cardstock; patterned paper (Dream Street); letter stickers, rub-on letters (American Crafts); chipboard animals (Magistical Memories); stamp (7gypsies); texture plates (Fiskars); Misc: chalk, floss, hole punch, ink

Technique *tip*

Don't have an embossing tool? You can fake it with one click using Photoshop Elements. Simply open an image and go to Filter>Stylize>Emboss.

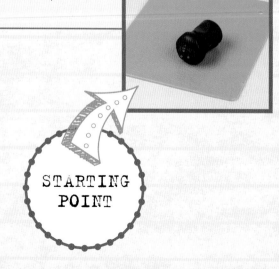

STARTING POINT

Oh yum!
I think a donut with icing
AND sprinkles brings a
smile to your face like not
many other foods can.
And who can blame you.
They are quite the treat.
I have to think though
that that smile is caused
not just by the
deliciousness of what you
are about to sink you
teeth into, but also by the
look of the donut itself. I
mean, how can you help
but smile when looking at
something just dancing
with little bits of color that
you are actually able
to eat.
Donuts are definitely a
treat for the eyes AND
the tummy.

with
Sprinkles
on top

Robby
Fall 2007

STARTING POINT

Tools made for scrapbooking are so convenient, but they can also be so inspiring when you look at them with fresh eyes. For this layout, I used a punch in an easy but unintended way. Creating sprinkles for my donut was tons of fun and easy to do by using the punched-out pieces left from a ribbon-glide punch. Think of other ways to use your scrapbook tools to inspire elements on your layout.

Supplies: Cardstock; patterned paper (Tinkering Ink); ribbon (Offray); Misc: Boopee font, corner rounder, ink, ribbon punch

Technique *tip*

Always look at both the negative and positive spaces of all your products for unique additions to pages. When using punches, save the cut-out paper for a frame; use what's left over from a sticker sheet as a stencil; or use punched-out holes to mimic brads.

Technique *tip*

There are so many ways to use letter stickers once the sheet is nearly empty. Use the negative space as stencils. Use your leftover Zs for a layout about sleeping. Add a monogram to a layout about someone special. Upside down Ws can stand in place of Ms. Create a polka dot pattern with periods.

Artwork by Kelly Noel

This layout makes me so happy. Not only does Kelly show us her sweet smiling son, but she is also inspiring us to use those leftover stickers from our alpha sticker sheets. What an adorable and clever way to both use up product and make an interesting layout. Look at your leftover supplies in new ways and use them as a starting point for your next page.

Supplies: Cardstock; patterned paper (MOD); buttons, chipboard and sticker accents, letter stickers (American Crafts); tab (7gypsies)

STARTING POINT

Monograms are timeless and popular elements, not just for scrapbook pages, but also in home décor. Single initials are often seen in home décor magazines and home furnishing catalogs. Ali's choice to use a stencil monogram as the primary element for her page about her home was, therefore, a natural one. Let a single letter guide the direction of a scrapbook layout and see where you are inspired to go.

Supplies: Cardstock; patterned paper (Creative Imaginations, Scenic Route); jumbo alpha (Bazzill); heart accents (American Crafts); Misc: Arial font

Artwork by Ali McLaughlin

Technique *tip*

Other fun ways to use a large letter on your layout include hinging the monogram to hide journaling, using it as a stencil or journaling directly onto the letter.

STARTING POINT

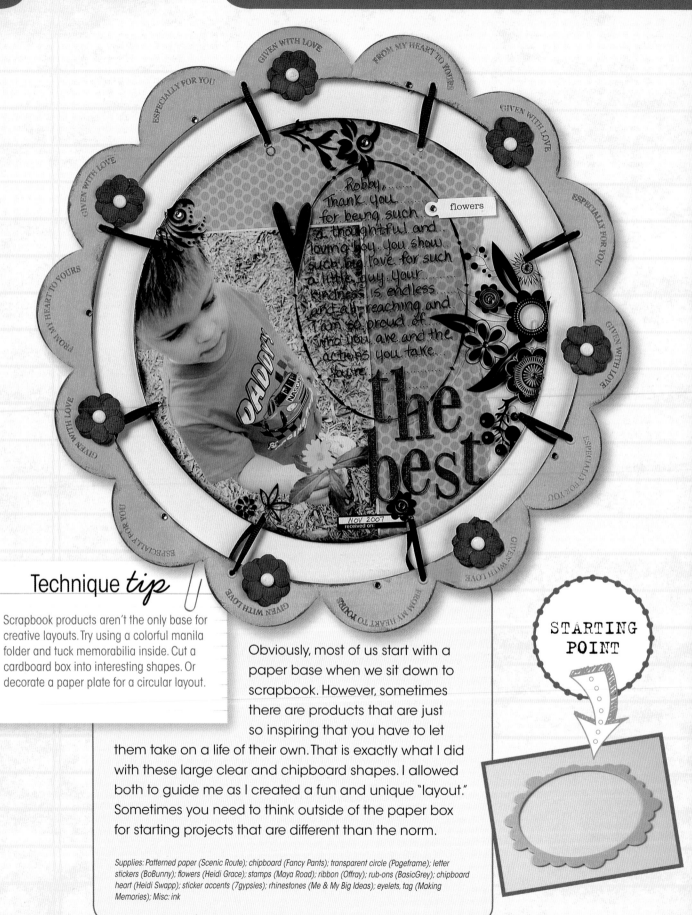

Technique *tip*

Scrapbook products aren't the only base for creative layouts. Try using a colorful manila folder and tuck memorabilia inside. Cut a cardboard box into interesting shapes. Or decorate a paper plate for a circular layout.

Obviously, most of us start with a paper base when we sit down to scrapbook. However, sometimes there are products that are just so inspiring that you have to let them take on a life of their own. That is exactly what I did with these large clear and chipboard shapes. I allowed both to guide me as I created a fun and unique "layout." Sometimes you need to think outside of the paper box for starting projects that are different than the norm.

Supplies: Patterned paper (Scenic Route); chipboard (Fancy Pants); transparent circle (Pageframe); letter stickers (BoBunny); flowers (Heidi Grace); stamps (Maya Road); ribbon (Offray); rub-ons (BasicGrey); chipboard heart (Heidi Swapp); sticker accents (7gypsies); rhinestones (Me & My Big Ideas); eyelets, tag (Making Memories); Misc: ink

STARTING POINT

I found that I was acquiring quite the collection of metallic scrapbook products and "bling" but having a hard time adding them to my layouts. I decided to let the sparkles be my guide. I picked my favorite pieces first and then chose my photos and story after that. By keeping the products I wanted to use on my layout in mind from the start, I was able to form a page in which they ended up fitting perfectly instead of being an afterthought.

Supplies: Cardstock; metallic paper (Die Cuts With A View); letter stickers, patterned paper (American Crafts); die-cut letters and shape (QuicKutz); paper frills (Doodlebug); bookplate (Heidi Swapp); rhinestones (Me & My Big Ideas); stamps (Inque Boutique); Misc: Garamond font, ink

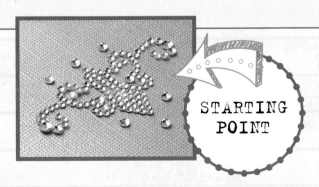

STARTING POINT

Technique *tip*

Don't have photos that you feel call for bling? Use the opportunity to create a layout without photos and use a little sparkle to make your page shine!

I never realized it before, but I think I go through phases when it comes to shapes that I am drawn to in décor and design. I find soft-cornered rectangles so attractive and pleasing to the eye. So I used a grouping I made of this exact shape as the starting point and main design element for this masculine page about the bond between my son and husband. Be inspired by the shapes that catch your eye and use these as a fun element on your layouts.

Supplies: Cardstock (Bazzill); dots, letter stickers (American Crafts); metal tag (Imaginisce); metal heart (Creative Imaginations); brads (Making Memories); Misc: Biondi, Dream Orphan and Machine Script fonts

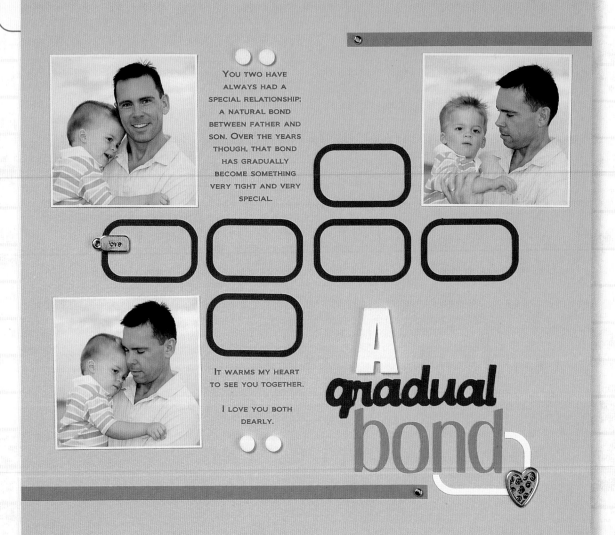

YOU TWO HAVE ALWAYS HAD A SPECIAL RELATIONSHIP; A NATURAL BOND BETWEEN FATHER AND SON. OVER THE YEARS THOUGH, THAT BOND HAS GRADUALLY BECOME SOMETHING VERY TIGHT AND VERY SPECIAL.

IT WARMS MY HEART TO SEE YOU TOGETHER.

I LOVE YOU BOTH DEARLY.

A gradual bond

Technique *tip*

Don't just use shapes on your layout, use them as your layouts. Step out of the box and do a layout in a shape other than a square or rectangle.

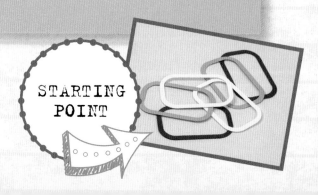

STARTING POINT

more like this

I am constantly craving more of this. More quality time for you and I. More times when we get to go out for an evening. More photos of us together during these times. More memories created of the great times you and I have together.

I can't get enough of spending time one-on-one with you. No matter how much we get, I will always be wanting ... more of this.

Supplies: Cardstock; die-cut shapes, letter stickers, patterned paper (BasicGrey); brads (Imaginisce); Misc: Impact font, corner rounder

Large elements and die-cuts aren't as easy to find as smaller embellishments. When I started scrapping this page, I knew I wanted a larger element to guide the design. To achieve this, I went on a hunt for a dingbat font that would be the perfect starting point. I selected a dingbat, enlarged it and printed it onto the back of patterned paper to cut and add to my layout.

STARTING POINT

DAILY GRIND

Your playtime has always had such purpose to it. You like to know that you are doing something that has a final result; an outcome you can be proud of. This holds true at home when you are doing your workbooks, helping with watering plants or completing a puzzle. Your behavior is no different when you are at Grammo's house. You enjoy finding jobs for yourself in her large yard and aren't afraid to work at them for hours. I enjoy seeing you gain so much pride in everything you do and hope that is something you carry with you through the years.

LIFE

STARTING POINT

I usually like the look of a photo frame to make photos pop off a layout. Most of the time a cardstock mat will do the trick, but sometimes a photo could use a little more help. For this layout, I added a digital frame prior to printing out the photo. Check out the abundance of digital frames available online as the inspiration for your next layout.

Supplies: Cardstock; patterned paper (BoBunny, Creative Imaginations); buttons (SEI); embellishments (EK Success); Misc: Georgia font, digital frame, floss

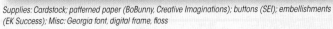

Supplies: Cardstock; die-cut shapes, patterned paper (Rusty Pickle); glitter letters (Making Memories); stamps (Inque Boutique); brads (Imaginisce); folded cards (Die Cuts With A View); Misc: ink

Note cards don't have to be just for sending. They also make convenient and colorful places to adhere photos and store journaling on a layout. Unlike a folded piece of cardstock, many note cards have a white interior that makes for the perfect place to add journaling. Use your leftover note cards on your layouts as a fabulous starting place for adding words.

STARTING POINT

Technique *tip*

Note cards come in such a fabulous variety of shapes, designs and colors. Search the stationery aisle of your favorite store for many cards to use as starting points.

Technique *tip*

Printing text directly onto stationery is easy. Type your text in a textbook in Word, making sure the box is smaller than the size of your stationery. Print the text onto regular paper. Use repositionable adhesive to attach the stationery to the paper over the printed text, and stick it back in the printer. Reprint the text so it prints onto the stationery paper.

I'M SORRY EASTER BUNNY, BUT IT WAS KIND OF HARD TO PAY ATTENTION TO YOU THIS YEAR. BLAME IT ON JEFF, CHRISTINE AND THE KIDDOS WHO BROUGHT OVER THE CUTEST NEW ADDITION TO THEIR HOME! WE WERE ALL INTRODUCED TO COCO AT GRAMMO'S HOUSE THIS YEAR AND SHE COULDN'T HAVE BEEN ANY CUTER! OUR ATTENTION WAS DEFINITELY ON A DIFFERENT LITTLE FURRY ONE.

COCO

STARTING POINT

When I first saw this stationery paper, it reminded me of the patterns and colors on some of my scrapbooking products. That fact probably played a big part in my purchase of it. So it was only natural that I put the sheets to use on a layout. The stylish paper served as the perfect place to hold the journaling for this layout about my brother's family and their new puppy. Look to stationery products for endless inspiration for interesting pages.

Supplies: Cardstock; patterned paper (My Mind's Eye); stationery (Vera Bradley); letter stickers (Making Memories); die-cut letters (QuicKutz); Misc: SP Sarahloo font

Technique *tip*

Want to keep your kids' photocopied coloring pages looking true to life? Copy the image onto off-white paper to mimic the color of paper in coloring books.

within the

Lines

Robby, Age 3

Speed Machine™

ROBBY

Crayola

CRAYONS

Bright and Vivid Colors!

8 Non-Toxic Crayons

As you approached turning three, your color turned from scribbles and random pictures on paper to more interest in coloring the fun illustrations found in color books. Daddy told you right from the start to try and stay inside the lines when you are coloring.

From the moment he said that, you took that bit of coloring advice very seriously. I don't think we ever saw a page in your books that had any crayon marks not within the lines they were intended. I am anxious to see where your rule-following and attention to detail take you in life.

I proudly admit that my love for crayons has followed me into adulthood. When I consolidate my son's crayons, I just can't bear to toss the fun and familiar boxes. For this layout showcasing one of my son's many colored pages, one of these boxes proved the perfect housing for my journaling. Think twice before tossing out items connected to something you may soon be scrapping.

STARTING POINT

Supplies: Cardstock; patterned paper (Tinkering Ink); brads (American Crafts); paper clip (Bazzill); crayon box (Crayola)

please **StOP** grow ing up so fast

1 month

6 months

years 1.5

years 2

Artwork by Summer Fullerton

I think it is so special when another craft or art form can be brought onto a scrapbook page. The handmade effect is so personal. Summer did a fabulous job of bringing the soft effect of watercolors onto this adorable layout about her godson. Think about what other crafts you enjoy and use those on a layout as the beginning of a page design.

Supplies: Cardstock (Bazzill); patterned paper (Jenni Bowlin); chipboard letters (We R Memory Keepers); acrylic shapes, rub-ons (American Crafts); chipboard numbers (Heidi Swapp); stickers (Arctic Frog); brads (Queen & Co.); Misc: paint, watercolors

How to *Use* it

Remember that products not intended for scrapbooking are not archival quality, so take extra care when using them. If you're concerned about keeping your photos well preserved when using found objects, make photocopies of photos and use the copies on layouts. If you use paper objects as inspiration and want to keep a layout well preserved, spray them with Archival Mist to make them acid free. Using adhesive—wet and dry—intended for scrapbooking is always a good idea no matter what kind of page you're making.

STARTING POINT

Artwork by Amy Licht

Kids' crafts are so much fun to do, even for us adults. It's no wonder that as we are creating, some of our kids' craft supplies would make it onto a scrapbook layout or two. On this layout, Amy turned ordinary craft pipe cleaners into pretty flowers, adding the perfect soft and feminine touch to the page. Think about what craft items your kids use regularly and see if you can't find one to inspire your own craft.

Supplies: Cardstock; patterned paper (Junkitz); pipe cleaners (Westrim); buttons (Autumn Leaves); decorative tape (Imagination Project); brads (Making Memories); rub-ons (American Crafts, K&Co.); Misc: Hootie, Plum Script and Uncle Charles fonts, felt ribbon, floss, tag

Technique *tip*

Try these other kids' crafts to make unique elements and embellishments for your own layouts: felt, modeling clay, colored chalk, beads, printable shrink sheets, construction paper and craft sticks.

STARTING POINT

cake & ice cream

IT'S VERY UNDERSTANDABLE WHY THE 'CAKE AND ICE CREAM PART' OF ANY PARTY IS YOUR FAVORITE. YOU LOVE YOUR TREATS AS MUCH AS ANY OTHER FOUR—YEAR—OLD. BUT THERE IS SOMETHING ABOUT THAT PART OF A PARTY THAT APPEALS TO US ADULTS TOO. EVEN IF WE AREN'T PARTICIPATING IN THE EATING, IT STILL HAS IT'S BENEFITS. CAKE AND ICE CREAM IS THE SIGNAL FOR EVERYONE (FOR THE MOST PART) TO FIND A SEAT AND ENJOY. IT'S THE PART WHERE YOU ARE WORN OUT FROM PLAY AND FROM GAMES. IT'S THE QUIET PART OF THE PARTY WHEN ALL THE FUN HAS BEEN HAD AND ANOTHER BIRTHDAY CELEBRATED.

Sewing is a trend that has made its way onto many of my scrapbook layouts. The multitude of colors of embroidery floss are an inspiring start to any layout that needs some soft texture or homespun charm. Try thinking beyond the stitch and use the floss to wrap around elements for a fun way to add texture and color.

Supplies: Cardstock; letter stickers, patterned paper (American Crafts); chipboard shapes (Heidi Swapp); mesh (Gotta Mesh); decorative scissors (Fiskars); Misc: Pea Sarahloo font, circle punch, floss, ink

STARTING POINT

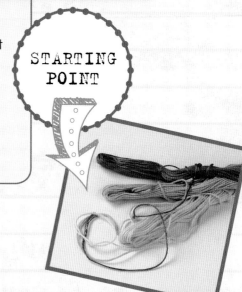

Technique *tip*

When using embroidery floss on your layout, don't forget to explore the many colors and textures floss now comes in. Why settle for white, when you can add some glittery silver or a rainbow-dyed variety?

I had these photos of my mom's wonderful birthday in the Bahamas for too long, as they sat without the perfect inspiration for a layout. Once I came across this leftover birthday tiara one day, I knew I had the perfect piece to guide the layout about this event. Party products prove festive starting points for layout designs, so have fun raiding your stash or taking a trip to the local party supply shop.

Supplies: Cardstock; patterned paper (Fancy Pants); word stickers (7gypsies); rub-on (K&Co.); Misc: Teen font, floss, ink, party hat

STARTING POINT

Technique *tip*

Festive inspiration doesn't have be party leftovers. Take a trip to the party supply store to find great starting points. Try cutting designs from paper plates or napkins or using tiny cake toppers as dimensional embellishments.

Artwork by Lisa Damrosch

wannabe style

1. It all started out so innocent. Simple braids & straight straight bangs. This worked for my early years, and then I wanted

2. Farrah hair so so badly. No amount of new fangled curling ironing could I get my straight straight bangs to feather. Thankfully

3. along came Dorothy Hammill & Short & straight was "in". I think that it is possible that for a day or so, I was "IN" too.

4. But then, the horrible, horrible mullett burst onto the scene, & onto my head for the vast majority of the early 80's

5. Somehow I believed that a BOY GEORGE look was an improvement & I tried all variations of Big hair until the early 90's

6. Unfortunately I think I have only myself to blame for "the poodle" of 1993, a style that will live on in infamy!

STARTING POINT

Lisa used the most fitting item as her embellishment on this layout: barrettes. What better way to inspire a fun and colorful layout about hair than hair-related product? Remember to think outside of the realm of scrapbook product for unexpected inspiration.

Supplies: Cardstock; patterned paper (Making Memories): chipboard letters (Heidi Swapp); ribbon (Offray); Misc: rickrack

---

festive family

You guys never fail to bring an enhanced sense of festiveness to the holidays. Tig's never-to-be-outgrown excitement for presents always adds a thrill to gift opening. Zob's role as scrooge is so falsely transparent that it is cute. And having Alex and Bobby around at the same time is always a welcoming sign that the holidays are here. (photo: Christmas 06)

I knew when I first saw these crafty snowflake ornaments that they would make their way onto a layout. Using the ornaments' obvious theme as my starting point, I paired them with a black-and-white photo to make the snowflakes the stars of the show.

Supplies: Cardstock; patterned paper (Tinkering Ink); chipboard shapes (Scrapworks); crocheted ornaments (Target); rhinestones (Me & My Big Ideas); Misc: Times New Roman font

STARTING POINT

THE PURCHASE OF THIS SHIRT WE BOUGHT YOU FROM THE GAP HELPS TO GET MEDICINE TO AIDS VICTIMS IN AFRICA. THIS IS JUST ONE CAUSE YOU MAY CHOOSE TO SUPPORT WHEN YOU GET OLDER. "CHARITY SHOULD BEGIN AT HOME, BUT SHOULD NOT STAY THERE" —Phillips Brooks

HOPE
DREAM
REACH OUT
SERVE OTHERS
BE KIND
SLOW DOWN

FALL '07

STARTING POINT

Kids' clothes are so adorable. Sometimes the tags and packaging on some of the items are as cute as the clothes themselves. That was definitely the case on this shirt I bought my son. After cutting the tag off the garment, I just couldn't throw it away. It became the starting point for a layout I created about my son wearing the shirt. Use product packaging to work as both embellishment and inspiration for a layout.

Supplies: Cardstock; patterned paper (My Mind's Eye, Scenic Route); denim pocket, letter stickers (Making Memories); metal arrow, tag, word stickers (7gypsies); jersey numbers (EK Success); peace brad (Around the Block); stencil tag (Autumn Leaves); word tag (Pebbles); metal clip (Karen Foster); bookplate (BasicGrey); rub-on (Hambly)

Technique tip

Tags don't have to be used as is on layouts. For example, cover a chipboard tag with patterned paper or paint. Use a shaped tag as a stencil. Flip a tag over and use it as a journaling box.

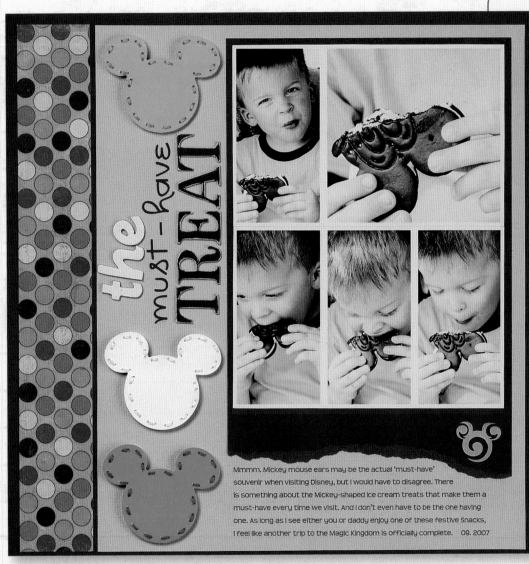

the must-have TREAT

Mmmm. Mickey mouse ears may be the actual 'must-have' souvenir when visiting Disney, but I would have to disagree. There is something about the Mickey-shaped ice cream treats that make them a must-have every time we visit. And I don't even have to be the one having one. As long as I see either you or daddy enjoy one of these festive snacks, I feel like another trip to the Magic Kingdom is officially complete.   09. 2007

When I came across these adorable paint chips at a local home improvement store, I couldn't resist picking up a few extra. I just knew I would have to use them in some way with some recent photos I had from a trip to Disney World. After using the paint chips for choosing a color for my son's bedroom, I cut out the Mickey symbol, hand stitched around the perimeter, and adhered them to my layout with adhesive foam. Products with fun symbols and shapes are all around, so keep an eye out!

Supplies: Cardstock; patterned paper (My Mind's Eye); chipboard letters (American Crafts, Heidi Swapp); metal clip (EK Success); Misc: Teen font, floss

STARTING POINT

Technique *tip*

Can't find paint chips in a fun shape? Use a standard paint chip and your favorite punch to create any shape you desire.

cutie

Yep, that's exactly what it says, Abby...and your daddy and I couldn't agree more! MARCH 2006

4

Doesn't that look interesting ?

Starting your pages with other inspirations

The world is filled with an abundance of attractive and inspiring sights. We see them in our everyday lives at stores, in magazines and as we travel. We bring them into our lives by collecting them, decorating with them or wearing them. It's not that unusual, then, that these things would inspire our layouts.

Unlike products that we use on our layouts, the items in this chapter act simply as inspiration. Whether it is an entire object or a small part of it, any item that catches our eye or speaks to us can serve as a source of scrapbook inspiration. I find inspiration pieces to be excellent starting points for layouts, as they can inspire everything from design to words to images. Let me show you how things all around can inspire the start of a layout.

I can't begin to express how invigorating it is to live a life aware of the details around me. I find myself inspired by so many things in my life. I am inspired by colors I see, textures I feel, sounds I hear and scents I smell. I am inspired by moods and weather and feelings. I find inspiration from people who are the closest to me and some that I have never met. I feel so alive living a life open to outside inspirations. It allows me to feel like I am involved in life and not just passing through. I am inspired and can't imagine my life any other way.

inspired

The moment I saw this greeting card, I was inspired. Unlike most items from which I gather inspiration, I utilized most of the elements on this card when creating my layout. I love the sherbet colors, the graphic angles, the contrasting shapes, and the pop of the black lettering. Greeting cards can provide endless inspiration in color, design, shape and sentiment.

Supplies: Cardstock (Bazzill); buttons (Blumenthal); Misc: Teletype font, floss

Technique *tip*

Greeting cards provide such a variety of inspirations! Don't have time to browse your local card store? Head online or pull out your old cards.

STARTING POINT

Supplies: Cardstock; patterned paper (Scenic Route, Tinkering Ink); die-cut letters (QuicKutz); flocked word (Making Memories); stamps (Inque Boutique); Misc: Century Gothic font, ink

I loved everything about this coaster when I saw it, so I wasn't sure where to begin when translating it to my layout. I decided to use the grid as a starting point, but basically copied the whole thing! I added a few fun photos, some stamps and journaling, and voila! a bright and fun layout.

STARTING POINT

Technique *tip*

To make a clean and finished look on any kind of layout, cover the gridlines and spaces between elements with thin strips of cardstock or ribbon.

What a gift Kelly has given with this tissue paper-inspired page. I love the way she paired the fun photos and journaling of her son with vivid circle designs picked up from the tissue paper. Gift wrap comes in so many styles and themes, there is sure to be one that would be a great start for your next design.

Artwork by Kelly Noel

go ahead, make a → mess

Supplies: Cardstock (Bazzill); patterned paper (American Crafts, KI Memories); chipboard, stickers (American Crafts); Misc: Digs my Hart and National Primary fonts, paint

STARTING POINT

Technique *tip*

Before cleaning up after a party or holiday, save a swatch of each wrapping paper and put it into an inspiration journal.

MARCH 2006

Yep, that's exactly what it says, Abby...and your daddy and I couldn't agree more!

cutie

cutie

STARTING POINT

Here, Amy turned a very cute shirt design into a page title. Amy's creative title adds both color and a personal touch. And now, her daughter's old T-shirt will be remembered for years to come.

Supplies: Cardstock; patterned paper (Anna Griffin, SEI); brads (Making Memories); ribbon (May Arts, Michaels); rub-on stitches (K&Co.); Misc: American Typewriter and Hootie fonts, photo corner

Artwork by Amy Licht

Fabulous parents who raised two wonderful kids.
Fun individuals who are as thoughtful to others are they are to each other.
Smart and active adults who know how to balance the important things in life.

They don't know it, but I look up to these two for these and so many more reasons.

these 2

Rob and Tig

(photo: 11.05 / journaling: 12.07)

STARTING POINT

I'm attracted to the look of mosaic tile; I like the mix of shapes and colors. So I couldn't help but use my mosaic pot as a starting point for this page. Mimic designs that move you to create pages that display what or who you love.

Supplies: Cardstock; chipboard shape (Fancy Pants); chipboard number (Rusty Pickle); fabric letters (Scrapworks); tag (QuicKutz); stamps (Inkadinkado); Misc: Teen font, ink

notes

These are that one pair of each of our shoes that seem to have a permanent place by our front door. You know the ones. The dog-walking, mailbox-checking, watering the plants and taking out the garbage slip-on shoes. Yep, these are those.

The Harrisons   Fall 2006

slip on s

I am constantly drawn to the familiarity and timelessness of classic patterns like argyle, houndstooth and plaid. One such pattern was my starting point for this layout about the small pile of shoes that remain at our front door. Not only did I use a patterned paper that was plaid, but I re-created the pattern using strips of cardstock. Think of your favorite patterns when in need of a creative starting point for a layout.

Supplies: Cardstock; patterned paper (BoBunny); jumbo letters, photo anchor (BasicGrey); chipboard letters (Heidi Swapp); brads (BoBunny, Making Memories); Misc: Franklin Gothic Book font, paint

STARTING POINT

Technique *tip*

Don't have patterned paper in your favorite pattern? Make a scan or color photocopy of fabrics around your house like those on shirts, washcloths and blankets.

I think it is because you get so excited when she visits us. Or maybe it is your way of putting on a little show. Whatever the reason may be, you sure do enjoy getting silly around your Aunt Ally. You make her work for every hug and picture she tries to get. Good thing she is so persistent...and very patient.

I am often inspired by interesting colors and patterns. For this layout, I was inspired by a patterned paper design and used a copy machine to enlarge the pattern to create a stencil. That stencil was the starting point for my layout's design. Many times, if you just take a moment to look within the patterns of your supplies, you will find great inspiration that will lead to fun and unexpected results.

Supplies: Cardstock (Bazzill); letter stickers, patterned paper, rub-ons (American Crafts); Misc: Traveling Typewriter font

Technique *tip*

Take a second look at the patterned paper you have in your stash. Even if you don't want to use the paper on your page, look for a design that catches your eye and use that to inspire your layout.

STARTING POINT

Technique *tip*

Copy everyday objects into smaller or larger images than they actually are. Use these as templates for designs on your layouts.

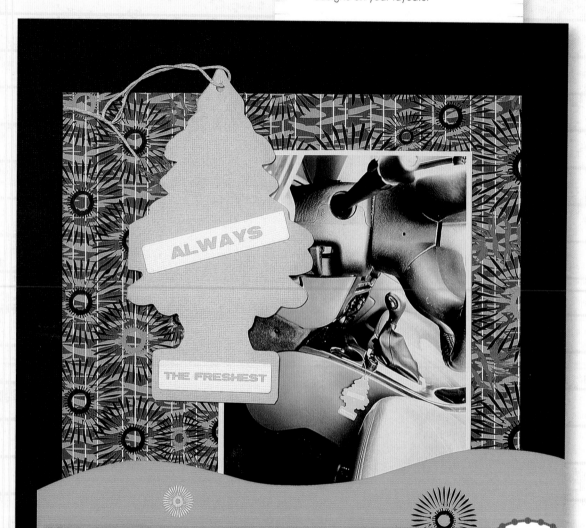

ALWAYS

THE FRESHEST

STARTING POINT

It was only a matter of time until one of these famous air fresheners made its way onto one of my layouts. My husband has made them such a part of our everyday life. As he was vacuuming his SUV one day, I couldn't help but get out the camera and snap a shot of this all-too-familiar sight. That sweet-smelling tree became the starting point for this entire layout, both for the photo and journaling.

Supplies: Cardstock; patterned paper, rub-ons (Tinkering Ink); stamp (Inque Boutique); Misc: Impact font, ink

Artwork by Denine Zielinski

Easter with Brittany & Brianne.

Finally some snow in February.

Your first beach trip since you were 3 years old.

Enjoying Dad's new pool with Emily.

favorite 5 memories

The year 2007 is officially half way over, and we sure have made some fun memories so far. There have been cold, blustery winter days and long, hot summer days. We have spent some time outdoors and have also been trapped indoors. In all, it has been a pretty wonderful year. Not just because of the beach, the parties, the fireworks, or the snow fun, but because of the people that we have shared our year with. It is our friends and family that have helped to make not only this year, but our lives, so joyous. So here's to being grateful for a super first half of 2007 and to hoping that the second half is just as great...if not better!

July 4th at the Thomas' house.

Supplies: Cardstock; patterned paper (KI Memories); brads (Making Memories); letter stickers, rub-on letters (American Crafts); Misc: AL Uncle Charles font, chipboard numbers

Denine did a fantastic job taking a page from a magazine that I would've flipped right past and turning it into a layout that makes me stop in my tracks. Her page, counting down favorite memories from the year, is a creative take on the magazine page and a great way to add multiple pictures to a layout. Magazines are endless sources for inspiration, from design and layout to concepts and color.

STARTING POINT

Technique *tip*

Try one of these magazine-inspired concepts on your next page: Interview a loved one. List your five favorite products. Print e-mails from special people for a Letters to the Editor-inspired page.

Artwork by Lisa Damrosch

Lisa isn't just celebrating being thirty-nine, but also the clever ideas she picked up from this cute gift bag. I adore Lisa's photo, the horizontal strips of words, and—my favorite part—the tucked-in journaling with part of the title dangling as a tag. Gift bags and tags are a fantastic source for inspiration with their ever-growing variety of shapes, themes and colors.

Supplies: Cardstock; patterned paper (Jenni Bowlin, KI Memories, Sassafras Lass, Scenic Route); letter stickers, rub-on letters (American Crafts); tag (Jenni Bowlin); flower (Doodlebug); brads (Bazzill); Misc: ribbon

STARTING POINT

Technique *tip*

Gift tag inspired titles (like Lisa's "I Am") can be used on any layout. Simply cut out 2–3 circles in different sizes and colors and then stack the circles. Punch a hole in the top and thread ribbon through. Add your title and you're done!

After meeting and falling in love with your Daddy, I didn't think there was too much more I needed in life. I knew I *wanted* a child, but I didn't think I *needed* a child. That is until you came along. In five years you have enhanced my life more than 100 years lived without you ever could. I am forever changed by the joy of having you in my life, by experiencing who you are already and with finding out who it is you are becoming. You are a gift I never knew I needed, but one that I now know I could never have lived without.

Supplies: Cardstock; patterned paper (Tinkering Ink); Misc: heart charm, ribbon

I stumbled across a free gift-wrapping service at a nice department store one holiday season and my view of wrapping was forever changed. The sight of that package never left my mind, and I knew it was only a matter of time before I had to re-create the look in some way. That's exactly where the starting point for this layout came from, and I just love the outcome in its elegant simplicity. Take a trip to the gift-wrap department next time you're out shopping to look for great layout inspiration.

How to *Inspire* it

It's important to remember that one piece of inspiration can inspire in so many ways. Don't forget to explore all the senses when examining an object of inspiration. It's a cinch for you to see inspiration in patterns, colors, design and shape. But take note of your other senses. How does the scent and feel of an object inspire you? Can the sounds around you inspire a page? How about the taste of food? Heighten your senses and you will never be at a loss for inspiration.

STARTING POINT

EVEN IN A PHOTO, THE SIGHT OF YOU COMPLETELY CRACKING UP MAKES ME SMILE. I CAN'T HELP MYSELF. WHEN YOU LAUGH HARD, YOU LAUGH FROM THE INSIDE OUT. EVERY BIT OF YOU SHINES AND IT APPEARS AS IF YOUR ENTIRE BODY IS GRINNING. ALL I KNOW IS I AM TOTALLY GUILTY OF DOING ALL THAT I CAN TO GET YOU IN THIS STATE AS OFTEN AS POSSIBLE. TO SAY YOUR HAPPINESS IS CONTAGIOUS WOULD BE AN UNDERSTATEMENT.

complete elation

I just love the combo of light cool colors with rich, chocolatey brown. That color scheme, along with a towel I have in my home, inspired the design for this layout. The designs and colors in your home are a good indication of what speaks to you, so take a look around the next time you need some design inspiration.

Supplies: Cardstock; patterned paper (American Crafts); plastic letters (Heidi Swapp); chipboard accents (Fancy Pants); rhinestones (Me & My Big Ideas); Misc: Noodle Script and Pea Sarahloo fonts, paint

STARTING POINT

Technique *tip*

Home décor inspiration can be found in a variety of places. Check out home décor magazines, home shows on TV, home décor Web sites and furniture catalogs to gain inspiration.

Artwork by Lisa Damrosch

Lisa flawlessly re-created the masculine look of a package of gum on this cool layout. I love how the subject matter and the design both suggest the future. For a fitting starting point, look at packaging on products that are geared toward the age or gender of your subject.

Supplies: Cardstock; patterned paper (CherryArte, Scenic Route); chipboard letters, clock accents (Heidi Swapp); brad (Queen & Co.)

STARTING POINT

When I'm in the shower, I'm washing my hair. When Kim is in the shower, she's getting inspired. And who can blame her when an everyday shampoo bottle turns into a positively endearing layout like this. Learn to look at ordinary items with a creative eye.

Supplies: Cardstock; patterned paper (Dream Street); chipboard heart (Heidi Swapp); rhinestones (Westrim)

STARTING POINT

Artwork by Kim Moreno

I am a sucker for cool title treatments, and this one by Summer is sheer perfection. Although Summer's inspiration started with a clever business card, she expanded on the original idea beautifully by using dimensional layered letters in two contrasting finishes. Bring your two-dimensional inspirations into the third dimension with a variety of textures and sizes.

Artwork by Summer Fullerton

Supplies: Cardstock; patterned paper (BasicGrey, My Mind's Eye); chipboard snowflakes, letter stickers (American Crafts); glitter letters (Making Memories); Misc: Geo Sans Light font, corner rounder, thread

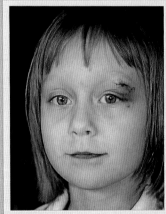

It started innocently enough as an afternoon excursion of sledding. The snow was thin but we managed to find what we thought was the perfect place. The kids were in heaven throwing snowballs and zooming down the hill. Then in a blink of an eye you went right into the base of a tree. When we fished you out we noticed in your battle versus nature, nature had won. You had a nasty cut above your right eye. Not only was it bleeding but it was filled with dirt and debris, a generous gift left behind by the tree. We quickly packed up and took you to a local urgent care facility where they cleaned you up and gave you stitches. Although the doctor thoughtfully stitched you up with a special plastic surgery stitch you will probably always have a mark above your eye and when you ask about it you will always be reminded of your brief and unsuccessful battle versus nature. February 2006

STARTING POINT

Technique *tip*

Use all kinds of elements from business cards for design inspiration. Copy color and fonts or mimic the look of the logo.

Technique *tip*

When transferring paint brochure ideas onto your layout, be sure to note the proportion of each color used and use a similar proportion on your layout.

Oh how this photo cracks me up! I mean, really. Does this look like we were having a fabulous vacation? No? Really? You don't see the happiness in our faces? Seriously though, this photo does bring back some great memories. This was taken when mom, dad and I went to Stone Mountain in Georgia. (Rob and Jeff were back home working, I believe.) I was in middle school so I must have been about twelve here, I think. I actually remember this photo being taken. Dad had just asked a guy if he would take our picture for us. We had just got to the top of Stone Mountain. We kept scooting back further towards the edge to get the landscape in the background. It was an extremely hazy day (obviously), but it didn't do much for the glare of the sun that still filtered through the clouds and into our eyes, (again, obviously). I really only remember bits and pieces from this trip. But what I remember is all happy and all good. I know, hard to believe with a souvenir photo like this one to show for it. Honestly though, this was a nice vacation for me with mom and dad. Because of this trip, I have even made a mental note for Rob and I to take Robby to Stone Mountain one day. Hey, if we are lucky, maybe we will end up with a similar photo to remember out trip by!

We can only hope!

Really, we were having a great time

Supplies: Cardstock; die-cut accent, patterned paper (Tinkering Ink); chipboard and plastic letters (Heidi Swapp); Misc: Teen font

I really like unexpected color combinations, so when I came across the paint brochures at my local home improvement store, I couldn't help but be inspired by the latest in home décor. I took home this brochure and went through my supply stash searching for elements in pink, red and blue. With the endless amount of paint color options available, you will find tons of color inspiration wherever you buy your paints.

STARTING POINT

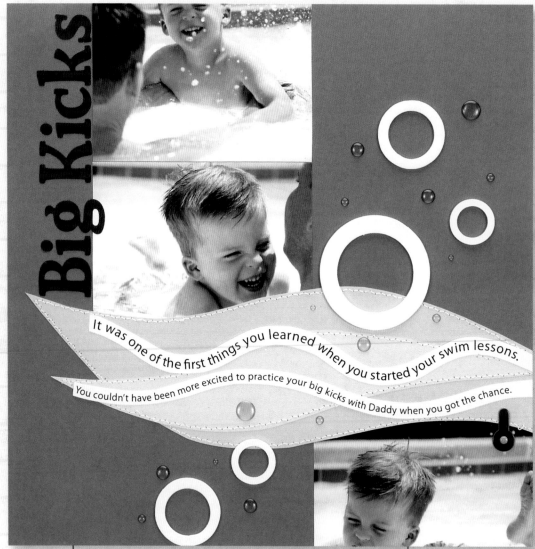

Big Kicks

It was one of the first things you learned when you started your swim lessons.

You couldn't have been more excited to practice your big kicks with Daddy when you got the chance.

When I first saw the wavy text and floating bubbles on this creamer ad, I was instantly inspired by the movement. My mind went directly to water since it was during the time my son had started learning to swim. The movement of the elements in the ad was a perfect start to a page about my son in the pool. In addition to words and shapes, let the movement of elements guide the way on your next layout.

STARTING POINT

How to *Inspire* it

It seems obvious, but it bears repeating: You can't inspire a layout without any inspiration. Taking photos of things that catch your eye as you go throughout your day is a great way to provide a treasure trove of inspiration. Carry around a point-and-shoot camera in your purse—and don't forget to use it! Your camera phone also works in a pinch. The great thing about inspiration photos is that they can not only inspire a layout but can also be used on a layout. To keep inspiration close at hand, organize your photos in an "inspiration" folder, either printed or on your hard drive.

Supplies: Cardstock (Bazzill); die-cut letters (QuicKutz); circle accents (Technique Tuesday); dot accents (Cloud 9); photo anchor (KI Memories); Misc: Arial font

On the layout:

R
O
B
E
R
T

I can't seem to ever be able to fully express how much you mean. I have been trying my best to do so, but it seems that words are so miniscule compared to the feelings I connect with them. With words not quite doing it, I have learned to further rely on my actions to show you know how much I love you and how much you are appreciated. I'm sure that you understand what you mean to me, but that doesn't make it any less important for me to continue to show you and tell you. I couldn't ask for more in a husband, a friend and a father. Each year you make me even more proud of who you are and what you do for me and our family. Always remember that even if you understand how I feel for you from my words and my actions, that my love for you will always be more than I could ever express.

I ♥ U

STARTING POINT

Unique architecture often catches my eye when visiting a new town, or even wandering a little in my own town. For the design of this layout, I was thoroughly inspired by the façade of a local theater. And who better to have the starring role than my wonderful husband. Visit the historic district or downtown of your own city to find inspiration from the shapes and designs of the surrounding sights.

Supplies: Cardstock; patterned paper (Tinkering Ink); chipboard letters (Heidi Swapp); brads, star (Making Memories); ribbon (Offray); Misc: Traveling Typewriter font, tag

Technique *tip*

It can be tricky to translate the design of a whole building onto a layout. To make the process simpler, take a photo of the building and then study it with a detailed eye, looking just for single shapes like triangles, circles or lines.

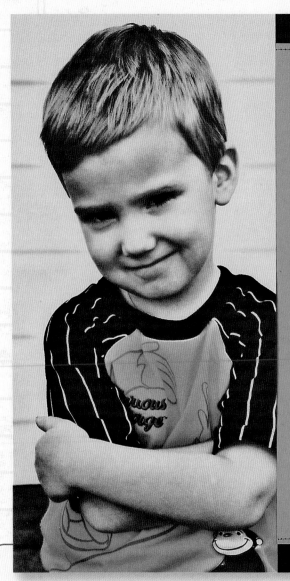

Holden, Summer 2006

The
only
kisses
I like are
HERSHEY'S
kisses

Supplies: Cardstock; Misc:
Abadi MT Condensed Extra
Bold, Arial Rounded, Bernard
MT Condensed, Century
Gothic and CrayonE fonts,
corner rounder, thread

Artwork by Lisa Moorefield

Lisa has achieved the impossible by giving me the only reason
why I wouldn't eat a piece of chocolate: to use it as inspiration
for a sweet layout like this one. Lisa cleverly transformed a
chocolate candy shape into a fun way to journal. Don't be
so quick to pop your favorite treat into your mouth; it may just
serve up a delicious starting point for your next layout.

STARTING
POINT

Technique *tip*

You can incorporate candy names
and packaging in so many fun ways
on a page. Use a Kit Kat bar on a
layout about your cat, a Tootsie Roll
as inspiration for a layout about feet,
or Smarties for a layout about your
straight-A kid.

Extra! Extra! Lisa has created an engaging layout inspired by a newspaper. Starting with a proven design like that of a newspaper article ensures a successful layout. The simplest of items can make for the cleverest of starting points. Take a second look at your everyday items when searching for inspiration.

Granddaughter Fires Her Papaw

NC – Scarlett fired her Papaw on New Year's Eve 2006 after he failed to play with her continuously.

Witnesses say that Papaw abandoned playtime with his granddaughter to answer a telephone call.

Scarlett became agitated and exclaimed, "You're fired!"

"I can't believe she fired me," Papaw said, still in shock. "And on New Year's Eve."

Scarlett could not be reached immediately for comment, as she was busy looking for someone else to play with.

Job Opening
Papaw. Must play constantly. Position available immediately. No pay. Long hours. Call Scarlett.

You're Fired.

Artwork by Lisa Moorefield   Supplies: Cardstock; brads (Making Memories); Misc: Times font, thread

Technique *tip*

There is a reason that newspapers and magazines use the designs and fonts that they do. They are timeless and tested for ease of reading and for what attracts the eye. When all else fails, rely on the pros for design inspiration.

STARTING POINT

Not only did Summer find a notebook to jot down some inspiring ideas, she found one to be inspired by as well. Summer used the split colors and round center design from the cover to create a clean and fun layout about her daughter's kindergarten tradition. When choosing items that you use daily, find ones that will be as inspiring to you as they will be useful.

Artwork by Summer Fullerton

This is the story of Fuzzy

a kindergarten tradition

Every year Fuzzy spends a weekend full of adventures and snuggles with each kindergartner in Mrs. Noren's class. You patiently waited for 5 months before you were chosen to take Fuzzy home for the weekend. Then finally in February Fuzzy came to stay with us. We took him everywhere with us – you went to dance class and Fuzzy came along – you got your hair cut and Fuzzy came along – you went to your big brother's basketball game and Fuzzy came along. Your adventures were documented in a traveling journal and then shared with your entire class. 02/2005

meet fuzzy

Supplies: Cardstock; patterned paper (Making Memories, My Mind's Eye); letter stickers (American Crafts); bookplate (BasicGrey); buttons (Junkitz); Misc: AvantGarde font, beads, decorative scissors, floss

notes

STARTING POINT

Technique *tip*

Remember that there are no rules about how an object inspires you, and the connection doesn't have to be obvious. Find a design intriguing but not so keen on the color? Use your imagination!

It's crazy how fast life passes us by. I can't believe you are almost 13 years old. So independent now, I'm not ready for you to grow up.

blink of
an
eye

Glamour queen

Supplies: Cardstock; patterned paper (American Crafts, Creative Imaginations); rub-on letters, tulip shapes (American Crafts); sticker (7gypsies); Misc: Arial font

Artwork by Ali McLaughlin

I couldn't think of a more fitting motif for a layout about a growing up girl than the one that Ali chose for this layout. Sophisticated yet girly tulips and polka dots, found in a magazine, were a perfect starting place to highlight her daughter's growth. When looking at magazines and catalogs, don't look past the advertised products to lend a little bit of inspiration to your own designs.

Technique *tip*

You don't have to have a magazine in front of you to be inspired by it. Check out magazine Web sites and blogs—they're full of photos and ideas sure to inspire.

STARTING POINT

Technique *tip*

Take an everyday role and make it bigger and better for a fun and fitting scrapbook page. If your son likes to sing in the shower, create a layout a rock star would envy.

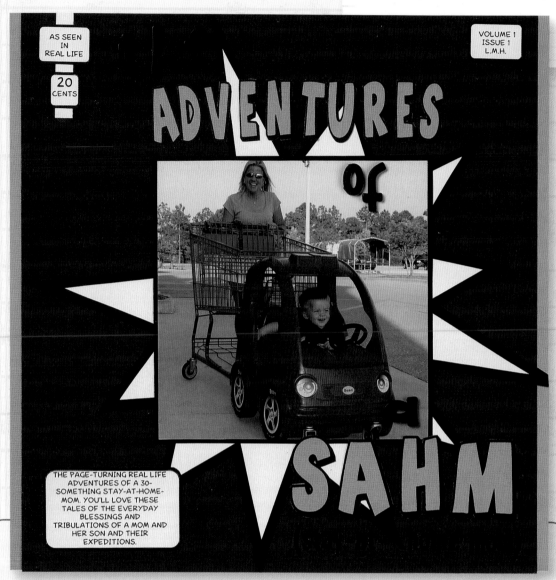

I would assume that every stay-at-home mom has had their moments when they felt like nothing less than a superhero. This feeling is exactly what flashed into my mind when creating a layout about my life as a stay-at-home mom. I used typical comic book elements as starting points for my design and continued the theme with font and color choices. It is fun to use fantasies as inspiration for what it is that we do in our daily lives.

Supplies: Cardstock; plastic letters (Li'l Davis); Misc: Comic Sans font

STARTING POINT

STARTING POINT

tough guy

I am beginning to realize that the simple joy of *having* the ball may just be your favorite part of playing football right now.

P·2007·SSESION

buddy

all boy

When I see football, the Gators come to mind. The University of Florida is a great local football team. Plus, my brother attended some time ago. So for this first football layout with my son, I used the colors of the team as a fitting color inspiration. Show team spirit on your sports layouts by using team colors as a starting point for your page.

Supplies: Cardstock; patterned paper (Sonburn); die-cut letters (QuicKutz); number stickers (Making Memories); epoxy stickers (SEI); photo turn (7gypsies); brads (Bazzill); Misc: Lucida Sans Unicode font, circle punches

Technique *tip*

Sports team and school colors don't have to inspire a sports-themed layout. For example, you can use the colors of your husband's alma mater as a starting point for a layout about his job.

Those annoying brightly colored lines that are found on TVs when there is no picture available used to be a nuisance to look at. Lately, the image seems to pop up more in modern advertising and culture. I used the idea of that image, but with a toned-down color palette, and created this layout about my little tough guy. Icons change with the times, but they're always great inspirations for layouts.

Supplies: Cardstock; letter stickers (American Crafts); die-cut icon (QuicKutz); stickers (7gypsies); Misc: chipboard letters, hole punch

Technique *tip*

Keep pen and paper nearby when watching TV. You can find a lot of inspiration in commercials, shows and movies.

STARTING POINT

Supplies: Cardstock; patterned paper (Tinkering Ink); letter stickers (Making Memories); book plate (Heidi Swapp); die-cut shape (QuicKutz); rub-on (7gypsies); Misc: Arial and Vila Moreno fonts

OBSERVATIONS
R o b b y
07

IT CLICKED

I hadn't realized it until Grammo got her new computer, that she hadn't seen you in action yet. In action on the computer, that is. You were already a wiz at playing preschool learning games on our computer at home, but we had yet to show Grammo what you could do. It was a pretty strange sight seeing you sit at Grammo's new computer, clicking away, knowing she had yet to learn as much about this technology as you already had a three-years-old. I only hope it will click for her as it has for you and maybe you will even be the one to help her to 'get it'.

It is easy to think of dingbats as generic symbols that wouldn't have much of a place on our pages. However, if paired with the right photos and fitting journaling, a well-placed symbol could be the perfect start for your next layout. I let the techno-inspired dingbat on the cover of this brochure be the guide when designing this modern page about my son's computer proficiency.

Technique *tip*

You can find lots of icons and dingbats for free. Check out the fonts and clipart that came with your word processing program or downlaod them from the Internet.

Switch

More talk, more savings.

(Comcast)

STARTING POINT

I WAS PRETTY THRILLED WHEN I CAME ACROSS THESE CHRISTMAS DISHES IN DECEMBER OF 2006. I WAS DOING A LITTLE LAST MINUTE GIFT SHOPPING AND FOUND THESE ON SALE FOR HALF OFF. THE SALE WAS ONLY A BONUS BECAUSE I WAS INSTANTLY SMITTEN WITH THESE AS A CHOICE FOR OUR HOLIDAY DISHES. THEY MATCHED SO MUCH ABOUT OUR FAMILY THAT I COULDN'T PASS THEM BY.

Every time I walk into a party store, I instantly want an excuse to throw a party just to use all the fabulous colors and textures of the decorations that are available. When I saw this plate, I was inspired to bring out my best dishes. Yes, they were the Christmas dishes, but this paper plate was the perfect inspiration for the font and title treatment for the layout. Party stores are chock full of endless inspirations that can work as festive starts for your layouts.

Supplies: Cardstock; patterned paper (Imaginisce); chipboard letters (Heidi Swapp); glitter letters (K&Co.); buttons (Jo-Ann's, SEI); circle shapes (Scenic Route, Xyron); Misc: Biondi and Marriage Script fonts, brad, glitter, tag

Technique *tip*

Party supplies can provide tons of inspiration. Look at how you can adapt fonts for your titles, images for your embellishments or colors for your page's scheme.

STARTING POINT

buffalo chicken salad

THIS MEAL IS SUCH AN EASY ONE TO MAKE, BUT IT IS STILL ONE OF ROB'S FAVORITES. TO MAKE, I CHOP UP SOME ICEBURG LETTUCE, CELERY, GREEN ONIONS AND PLUM TOMATOES. I PUT IT ALL INTO A BOWL AND TOP WITH RANCH DRESSING AND SHREDDED CHEDDAR. MEANWHILE, I SEASON SOME CHICKEN BREASTS AND GRILL UNTIL DONE. THEN I CUT UP THE CHICKEN, COAT WITH ROB'S FAVORITE WING SAUCE AND ADD TO SALAD.

I never thought of photographing my meals until I saw this book about a man who photographed every thing he ate for a year. Without the inspiration, I wouldn't have been inclined to make a layout about one of my husband's favorite meals. There are books on everything—get inspired!

Supplies: Cardstock; patterned paper (Sassafras Lass); letter stickers (Doodlebug); brads, metal charm (Karen Foster); ribbon (Offray); rub-ons (Tinkering Ink); trim (Rusty Pickle); Misc: circle punch, floss

STARTING POINT

Mrs. Claus

It was only fitting that on this layout about my mom's giving nature that I used elements inspired by her favorite holiday song, "Silver and Gold" by Burl Ives. Color inspiration doesn't need to come straight from a color source; songs can bring unexpected inspiration for layouts as well.

Supplies: Cardstock; patterned paper (Tinkering Ink); glitter stars (Blumenthal); mesh (Magic Mesh); Misc: Impact font, floss

STARTING POINT

Lisa Damrosch has been scrapbooking for as long as she can remember, and she now says that she can't imagine her life without it. Because of scrapbooking, Lisa has discovered a love for photography and a new and more creative view of the world around her. Lisa believes that inspiration is everywhere, and says that she most enjoys feeling "fearless" when she creates. Her rich and vibrant design style and love of storytelling keep her pages full of life. Nothing is off limits when it comes to the subjects she tackles or the product combinations she loves to experiment with. Lisa lives in the San Francisco Bay area with her husband Matt, her son Todd, and her big old Labrador Huckleberry.

Summer Fullerton began her creative journey at a young age as she grew up surrounded by inspiration. She received her first camera in 1976, and although it wasn't loaded with film until many years later, the seeds of artistry were planted. After the birth of her first child, Summer discovered scrapbooking as we know it today and has been hooked ever since. Her published creations can be seen in many scrapbook publications, and she was named to be in the 2007 Creating Keepsakes Hall of Fame. Summer lives with her husband of 14 years, Brad and her two children, Grant and Corinne, in Tigard, Oregon.

Amy Licht discovered a new passion and creative outlet in scrapbooking and photography in January 2004. A year later, after finding some success in submitting her pages for publication, she was selected to be on the 2007 BHG, Scrapbooks, Etc. Creative Team. She is blessed to have three active children who keep her very busy and are the inspiration for most of her designs. Amy is a former high school math teacher and has been married to her husband, John, for 11 years.

Ali McLaughlin has been scrapbooking for about seven years now. She has her best friends to thank, as they introduced her to the hobby. Ali's style is more on the simple side, but she loves adding pops of color to her pages and mixing fun patterns and embellishments. Since starting this hobby, she has had many wonderful publishing opportunities. She was named an Honorable Mention to the 2006 CK Hall of Fame, and got her first cover on the June 2006 issue of *Scrapbook Trends*. She loves being on her favorite manufacturer team, American Crafts, and kit club, Scarlet Lime. Ali enjoys photography, traveling and spending time with her family: husband, Mike, and two kids, Alexis and Evan.

Lisa Moorefield has been scrapbooking for about seven years, and she loves how it enables her to incorporate many other interests. She can piece together papers like a quilt, draw and paint, add a creative story with some family history, and sew it all together into one scrapbook page. Lisa and her husband live in North Carolina with their two children. Her starting point is usually Starbucks coffee.

Kim Moreno has been scrapbooking since around 2000. She has since designed for several manufacturers and has been published in a variety of magazines including *Creating Keepsakes, Memory Makers, Scrapbook Trends* and more. Kim is also a 2008 Memory Makers Master Runner Up. Kim enjoys knowing she is documenting memories for her children to look back on and enjoy when they are older.

Kim was born and raised in Texas. She married young to a military man, Jesse, and has since lived in several places. She is currently stationed in Tucson, Arizona. She is the proud mom of five little ones ranging in age from 11 to 5-year-old twins. Life is a bit crazy but loads of fun!

Kelly Noel started scrapbooking in college and it quickly became an obsession after her first son was born in 2004. She likes to scrapbook late at night when the rest of her family is asleep and finds the hobby to be such a great creative outlet for her. She really enjoys the photography aspect of scrapbooking as well and is almost never without her camera. Kelly was choosen to be in the 2008 CK Hall of Fame. She lives in Florida with her husband and their two sons.

Denine Zielinski began scrapbooking almost eight years ago right after the birth of her son. Her work has been featured in a variety of publications since 2004. She had the honor of being named a finalist in the 2006 Memory Makers Masters contest and she was named a 2008 CK Hall of Fame winner. She also served as a member of the Arctic Frog design team. Denine has always been a creative person dabbling in other crafts such as woodworking and sewing. She is a single mom and a high school teacher. She currently resides in Pennsylvania with her eight-year-old son, Ryan.

Source *guide*

7gypsies
(877) 749-7797
www.sevengypsies.com

A2Z Essentials
(419) 663-2869
www.geta2z.com

Adornit/Carolee's Creations
(435) 563-1100
www.adornit.com

American Crafts
(801) 226-0747
www.americancrafts.com

Anna Griffin, Inc.
(888) 817-8170
www.annagriffin.com

Arctic Frog
(479) 636-3764
www.arcticfrog.com

Around The Block
(801) 593-1946
www.aroundtheblockproducts.com

Autumn Leaves
(800) 588-6707
www.autumnleaves.com

Avery Dennison Corporation
(800) 462-8379
www.avery.com

BasicGrey
(801) 544-1116
www.basicgrey.com

Bazzill Basics Paper
(480) 558-8557
www.bazzillbasics.com

Beary Patch Inc.
(877) 327-2111
www.bearypatchinc.com

Berwick Offray, LLC
(800) 344-5533
www.offray.com

Blumenthal Lansing Company
(563) 538-4211
www.buttonsplus.com

BoBunny Press
(801) 771-4010
www.bobunny.com

Boxer Scrapbook Productions, LLC
(888) 625-6255
www.boxerscrapbooks.com

Canson, Inc.
(800) 628-9283
www.canson-us.com

Chatterbox, Inc.
(888) 416-6260
www.chatterboxinc.com

Chenille Kraft
(800) 621-1261
www.chenillekraft.com

CherryArte
(212) 465-3495
www.cherryarte.com

Cloud 9 Design
(866) 348-5661
www.cloud9design.biz

Crayola
(800) 272-9652
www.crayola.com

Creative Imaginations
(800) 942-6487
www.cigift.com

Daisy D's Paper Company
(888) 601-8955
www.daisydspaper.com

Dèjá Views
(800) 243-8419
www.dejaviews.com

Deluxe Designs—no longer in business

Designer Digitals
www.designerdigitals.com

Die Cuts With A View
(801) 224-6766
www.diecutswithaview.com

DMC Corp.
(973) 589-0606
www.dmc-usa.com

Doodlebug Design Inc.
(877) 800-9190
www.doodlebug.ws

Dream Street Papers
(480) 275-9736
www.dreamstreetpapers.com

Duncan Enterprises
(800) 438-6226
www.duncanceramics.com

EK Success, Ltd.
(800) 524-1349
www.eksuccess.com

Fancy Pants Designs, LLC
(801) 779-3212
www.fancypantsdesigns.com

Fiskars, Inc.
(866) 348-5661
www.fiskars.com

Flair Designs
(888) 546-9990
www.flairdesignsinc.com

Fonts101
www.fonts101.com

Fontstock
www.fontstock.net

Fontwerks
(604) 942-3105
www.fontwerks.com

Gotta Mesh
www.gottamesh.net

Hambly Studios
(800) 451-3999
www.hamblystudios.com

Heidi Grace Designs, Inc.
(866) 348-5661
www.heidigrace.com

Heidi Swapp/Advantus Corporation
(904) 482-0092
www.heidiswapp.com

Imagination Project, Inc.
(888) 477-6532
www.imaginationproject.com

Imaginisce
(801) 908-8111
www.imaginisce.com

Inkadinkado Rubber Stamps
(800) 523-8452
www.inkadinkado.com

Inque Boutique Inc.
www.inqueboutique.com

Jenni Bowlin
www.jennibowlin.com

Jo-Ann Stores
www.joann.com

Junkitz—no longer in business

K&Company
(888) 244-2083
www.kandcompany.com

Karen Foster Design
(801) 451-9779
www.karenfosterdesign.com

KI Memories
(972) 243-5595
www.kimemories.com

Kunin Group, The
(800) 292-7900
www.kuningroup.com

Li'l Davis Designs
(480) 223-0080
www.lildavisdesigns.com

Limited Edition Rubberstamps
(800) 229-1019
www.limitededitionrs.com

Magic Mesh
(651) 345-6374
www.magicmesh.com

Magic Scraps
(904) 482-0092
www.magicscraps.com

Magistical Memories
(818) 842-1540
www.magisticalmemories.com

Making Memories
(801) 294-0430
www.makingmemories.com

May Arts
(800) 442-3950
www.mayarts.com

Maya Road, LLC
(214) 488-3279
www.mayaroad.com

Me & My Big Ideas
(949) 583-2065
www.meandmybigideas.com

Michaels Arts & Crafts
(800) 642-4235
www.michaels.com

MOD — My Own Design
(303) 641-8680
www.mod-myowndesign.com

My Mind's Eye, Inc.
(800) 665-5116
www.mymindseye.com

Offray- see Berwick Offray, LLC

Pageframe Designs
(877) 553-7263
www.scrapbookframe.com

Paper Wishes by Hot Off the Press
(888) 300-3406
www.paperwishes.com

Pebbles Inc.
(801) 235-1520
www.pebblesinc.com

Prima Marketing, Inc.
(909) 627-5532
www.primamarketinginc.com

Provo Craft
(800) 937-7686
www.provocraft.com

Queen & Co.
(858) 613-7858
www.queenandcompany.com

QuicKutz, Inc.
(888) 702-1146
www.quickutz.com

Reminisce Papers
(319) 358-9777
www.shopreminisce.com

Rusty Pickle
(801) 746-1045
www.rustypickle.com

Sassafras Lass
(801) 269-1331
www.sassafraslass.com

Savvy Stamps
(866) 447-2889
www.savvystamps.com

Scenic Route Paper Co.
(801) 542-8071
www.scenicroutepaper.com

Scrapsupply
(615) 777-3953
www.scrapsupply.com

Scrapworks, LLC / As You Wish Products, LLC
(801) 363-1010
www.scrapworks.com

SEI, Inc.
(800) 333-3279
www.shopsei.com

Sizzix
(877) 355-4766
www.sizzix.com

Sonburn, Inc.
(800) 436-4919
www.sonburn.com

Stampin' Up!
(800) 782-6787
www.stampinup.com

Stemma/Masterpiece Studios
www.masterpiecestudios.com

Target
www.target.com

Technique Tuesday, LLC
(503) 644-4073
www.techniquetuesday.com

Three Bugs in a Rug, LLC
(801) 804-6657
www.threebugsinarug.com

Tinkering Ink
(877) 727-2784
www.tinkeringink.com

Two Peas in a Bucket
(888) 896-7327
www.twopeasinabucket.com

Vera Bradley
(888) 855-8372
www.verabradley.com

We R Memory Keepers, Inc.
(801) 539-5000
www.weronthenet.com

Westrim Crafts
(800) 727-2727
www.westrimcrafts.com

Wordsworth
(877) 280-0934
www.wordsworthstamps.com

Xyron
(800) 793-3523
www.xyron.com

FOR MORE INSPIRATION AND IDEAS, CHECK OUT THESE OTHER MEMORY MAKERS BOOKS

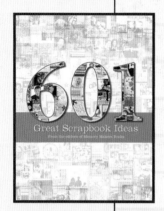

601 Great Scrapbook Ideas

Brimming with inspiration and ideas, you'll discover one amazing page after another in this big book of layouts.

ISBN-13: 978-1-59963-017-5
ISBN-10: 1-59963-017-6

paperback

272 pages

Z1640

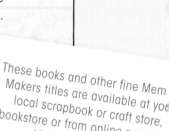

These books and other fine Memory Makers titles are available at your local scrapbook or craft store, bookstore or from online supplier. Visit our Web site at www.mycraftivity.com and www.memorymakersmagazine.com

Ask the Masters!
Making the Most of Your Scrapbook Supplies

Innovative and inspiring ideas from the Memory Makers Masters for using that growing stash of scrapbook supplies and tools.

ISBN-13: 978-1-59963-012-0
ISBN-10: 1-59963-012-5

paperback

128 pages

Z1040

Out of Bounds

Push the boundaries of your scrapbooking with creative inspiration and innovative ideas from leading scrapbook designers Jodi Amidei and Torrey Scott.

ISBN-13: 978-1-59963-009-0
ISBN-10: 1-59963-009-5

paperback

128 pages

Z0795

What About the Words?

Journaling on your scrapbook layouts is easy with the advice, examples and inspirations found here.

ISBN-13: 978-1-892127-77-8
ISBN-10: 1-892127-77-6

paperback

128 pages

Z0017

See what's coming up from Memory Makers Books by checking out our blog:

www.mycraftivity.com/scrapbooking_papercrafts/blog/